North Bay Ontario in Colour Photos, Saving Our History One Photo at a Time

Photography
by Barbara Raué
©2021

Series Name: Cruising Ontario

Book 210: North Bay

Cover photo: 610 Copeland Avenue, Page 42

©2021 All the photos in this book have been taken with my cameras. I own the rights to them.

Series Name: Cruising Ontario
Saving Our History One Photo at a Time
in colour photos

Books Available in Alphabetical Order:
Aberfoyle, Acton, Ajax, Alton, Amherstburg, Ancaster, Arthur, Auburn, Aylmer, Ayr, Beaver Valley, Belgrave, Belleville, Bloomingdale, Blyth, Brantford, Brockville, Burford, Burlington, Caledon, Caledonia, Cambridge, Carlow, Chatsworth, Clifford, Collingwood, Conestogo, Delhi, Dorchester to Aylmer, Drayton, Drumbo, Dundas, Dunlop, Eden Mills, Elmira, Elora, Erin, Essex, Fergus, Goderich, Grimsby, Guelph, Hagersville, Hamilton, Hanover, Harriston, Hespeler, Jarvis, Kingston, Kingsville, Kitchener, Lake Superior, Lincoln, Linwood, Listowel, London, Lucknow, Merrickville, Mono, Mount Forest, Mount Pleasant, Neustadt, New Hamburg, Newboro, Newport, Niagara-on-the-Lake, Niagara Falls, North Bay, Oakville, Onondaga, Orangeville, Orillia, Oshawa, Owen Sound, Palmerston, Paris, Pelham, Perth, Peterborough, Petrolia, Pickering, Port Colborne, Port Elgin, Portland, Preston, Rockwood, Sarnia, Sault Ste. Marie, Seaforth, Sheffield, Shelburne, Simcoe, Smiths Falls, Smithville, Southampton, St. Catharines, St. George, St. Jacobs, St. Marys, St. Thomas, Stoney Creek, Stratford, Thamesford, Thunder Bay, Tillsonburg, Toronto, Waterdown, Waterford, Waterloo, Welland, Wellesley, West Flamborough, Westport, Whitby, Windsor, Wingham, Woodstock

Book 201-202: Whitby
Book 203: Ajax, Pickering
Book 204-206: Oshawa
Book 207-209: Niagara Falls
Book 210: North Bay

Table of Contents

The Gateway Arch, Lee Park	Page 5
Second Avenue West	Page 7
Wyld Avenue	Page 8
Fraser Street	Page 10
Ferguson Street	Page 11
First Avenue West	Page 14
McIntyre Street West	Page 19
McIntyre Street East	Page 37
Algonquin Avenue	Page 40
Copeland Avenue	Page 41
Jane Street	Page 43
Durril Street	Page 46
Mclaren Street	Page 47
Bloem Street	Page 50
Front Street	Page 54
High Street	Page 55
McPhail Street	Page 56
Trout Lake Road	Page 58
Carousels	Page 60
Chief Commanda	Page 64
Beth Street	Page 68

North Bay is a city in Northeastern Ontario about 330 kilometers (210 miles) north of Toronto. It differs in geography from Southern Ontario because North Bay is situated on the Canadian Shield which results in a more rugged landscape. North Bay straddles both the Ottawa River watershed to the east and the Great Lakes Basin to the west. The city's urban core is located between Lake Nipissing and the smaller Trout Lake.

In 1882, John Ferguson decided that the north bay of Lake Nipissing was a promising spot for settlement. Apart from Indigenous people, voyageurs and surveyors, there was little activity in the Lake Nipissing area until the arrival of the Canadian Pacific Railway (CPR) in 1882. North Bay was selected as the southern terminus of the Temiskaming and Northern Ontario Railway (T&NO) in 1902 when the Ross government took the bold move to establish a development road to serve the Haileybury settlement. During construction of the T&NO, silver was discovered at Cobalt and started a mining frenzy in the northern part of the province that continued for many years. The Canadian Northern Railway was built to North Bay in 1913.

North Bay grew through a strong lumbering sector, mining and the three railways in the early days.

Born in France about 1598, Jean Nicolet, explorer, fur trader, and interpreter came to Canada in 1618. Under orders from Samuel de Champlain, he spent the following two years with the Algonquins of Allumette Island. He was then sent to the Nipissing Indians of this area and dwelt among them for at least eight years, learning their language, adopting their customs, and strengthening their alliance with the French. Nicolet is credited with the discovery of Lake Michigan which he explored as far south as the head of Green Bay in 1634. He later settled in Trois Rivieres. He drowned in the St. Lawrence in 1642.

The rivers and lakes of northern Ontario have been highways for travel and commerce for hundreds of years. First nations and European explorers used Lake Nipissing for transporting their furs. When the railroad reached the area in the 1880s, settlers and timber were transported across the lake.

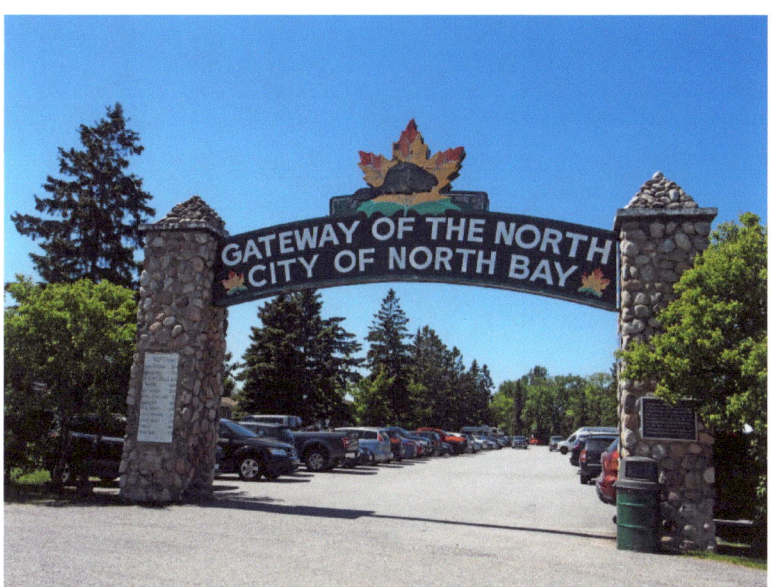

The Gateway Arch was constructed in 1928 and serves as an entrance to Lee Park. It is an important symbol of North Bay, the "Gateway City." The two pillars supporting the arch are made of large, rounded river stones that are held in place with cement mortar. The term and concept of "Gateway to the North" first appeared around the late nineteenth and early twentieth centuries. This term came about due to the realization that North Bay, because of its geographical location, was an inter-connecting link for both north-south and east-west traffic.

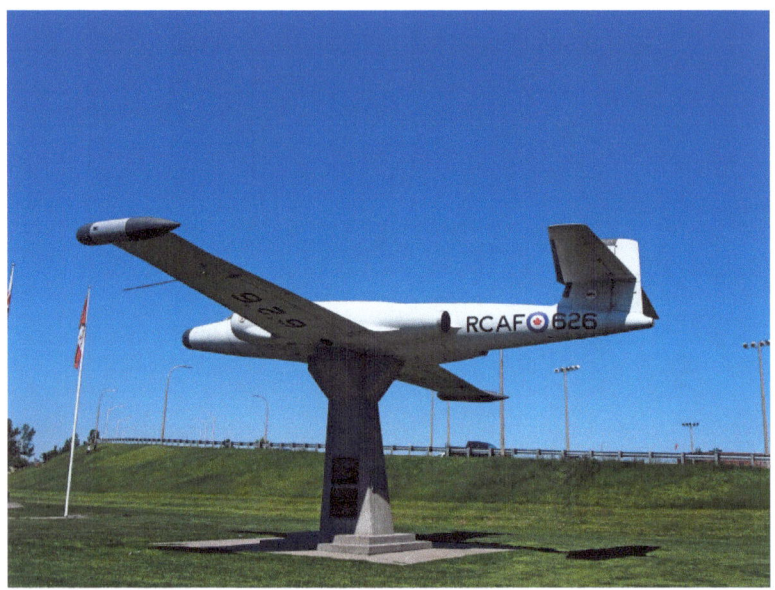

    The CF100 "Canuck" was conceived to meet the demanding requirements of defending a country as large as Canada. Its first flight was on January 19, 1950. There were nine squadrons of these planes based in Canada, four based in Europe, and three in Belgium. A total of 692 CF100s were built.

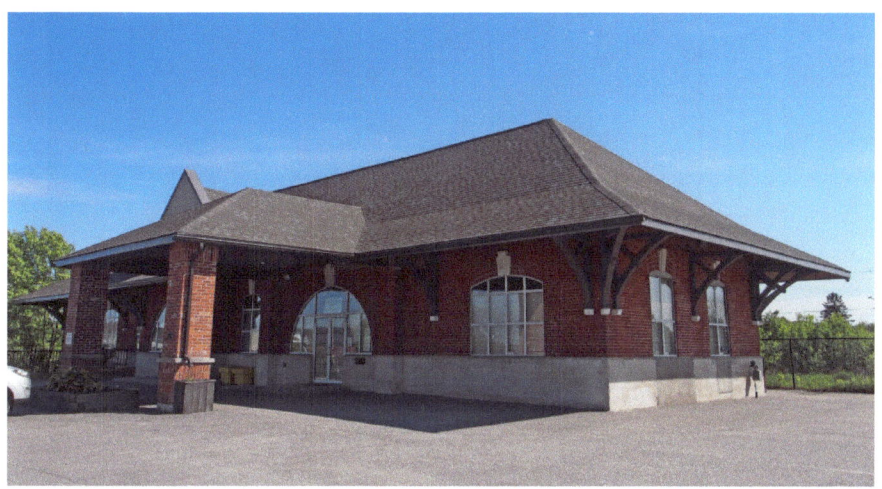

198 Second Avenue West - Former Canadian National Railway Station

The Timiskaming and Northern Ontario Railway (T&NO) extended their line from North Bay to New Liskeard in 1905 to serve the forestry, mining and agricultural resources of the northeastern area of the province. In 1911, the Grand Trunk Railway (GT) extended from Callander to North Bay with running rights negotiated over the T&NO all the way to Cochrane.

The Canadian Northern System (CNO) decided in 1914 to erect the existing station on their line through North Bay, then serving the CNO, GT, and the T&NO. With the ultimate extension of the T&NO to Moosonee, this completed the crossroads of North-South and East-West rail services from "coast to coast", geographically centered in North Bay.

The building has key stoned round-headed arches over the windows and doors with a slightly bell-hipped low roof line.

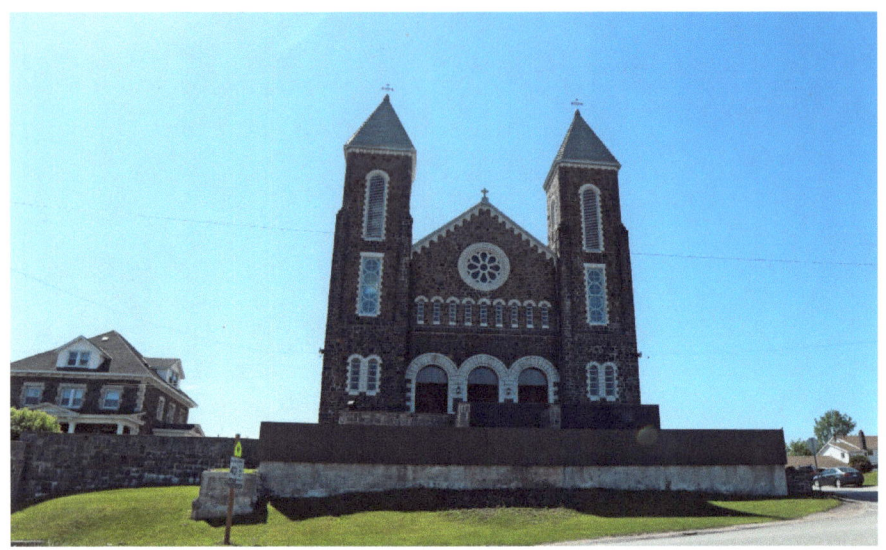

1265 Wyld Street - St. Vincent de Paul Roman Catholic Church – It is in the Romanesque style with the heavy massing achieved through the use of local cut stone, round headed arches over most openings, and the twin towers.

This is the first French Roman Catholic church constructed in North Bay. It was built in 1914 by Henri Marceau with the help of local parishioners. The original building was a simple basement with a low tin embossed ceiling. In 1932, a new superstructure was designed by B. A. Jones Architects from Kitchener, Ontario, which was built over the existing structure.

The commanding hilltop on which the church is built establishes this building as a visual landmark in the immediate community.

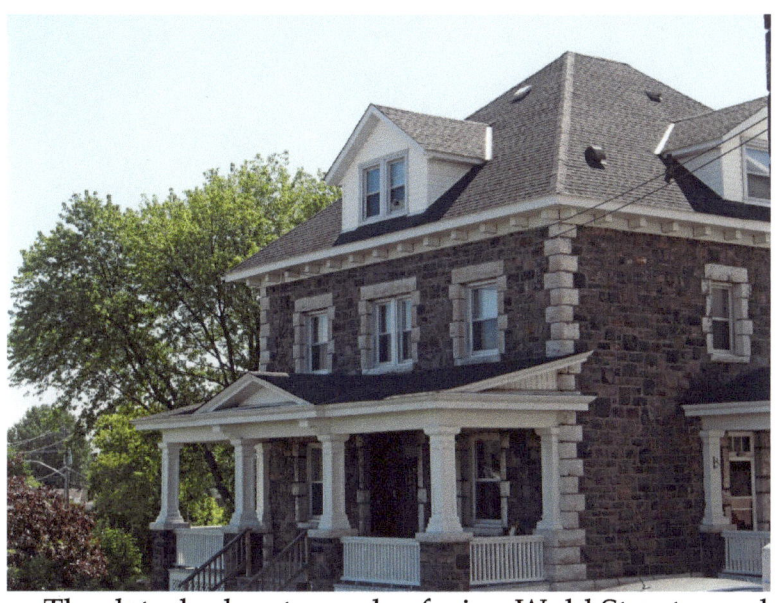

The detached rectory, also facing Wyld Street, employs matching materials that show the two buildings as one complex. Random patterned stone walls are used effectively to accommodate the building to the steep slopes of the front hillside.

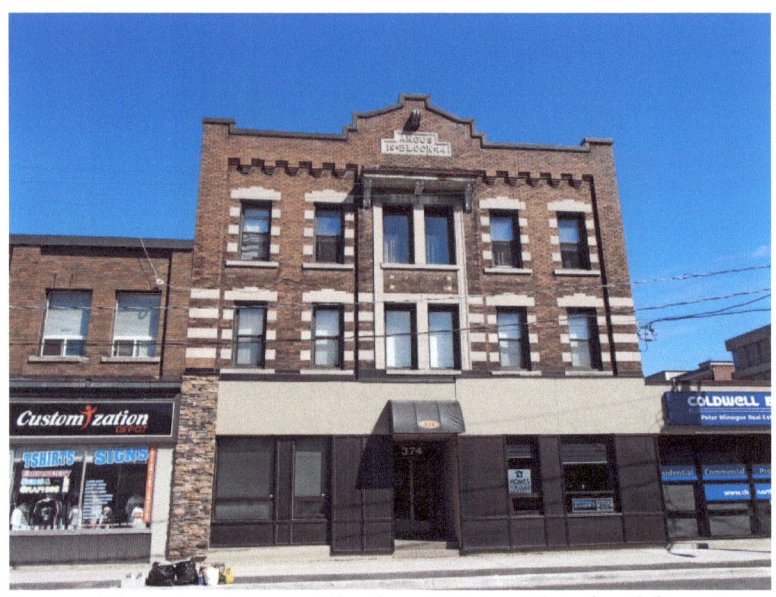

374 Fraser Street – Angus Block – 1914 – This building is noted for its parapet at the roof line and for its highly distinctive white stone window surrounds consisting of stepped lintels, quoined jambs and flat sills. Other notable features include the toothed heading of the in-stepped brick facing and bracketed canopy over the third floor paired openings. The date stone indicates that H.W. Angus, an early architect in North Bay, was responsible for its design and erection.

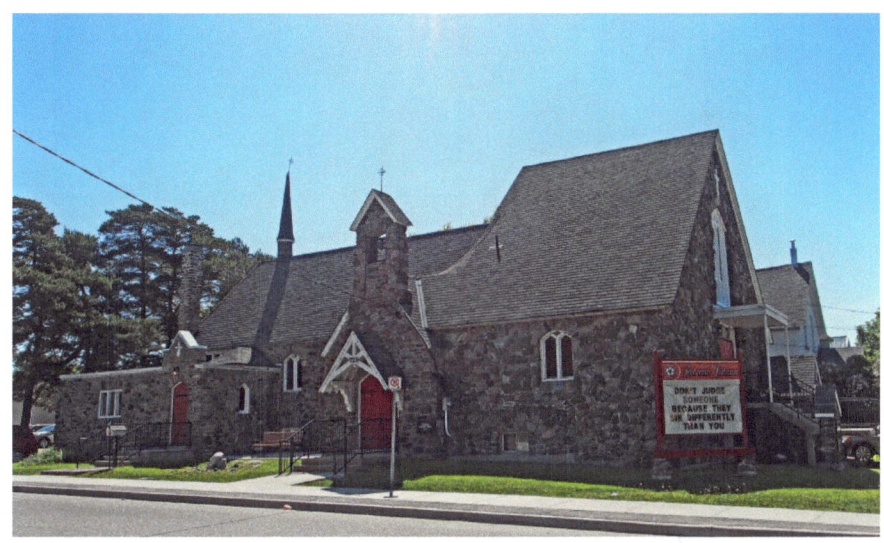

725 Ferguson Street – The Redeemer Lutheran Church fronts onto both Second Avenue and Ferguson. The location is adjacent to picturesque Memorial Park and the War Memorial.

Construction was completed in 1937. Native granite rock on the exterior of the building gives the church a unique appearance. The stone was not cut into traditional bricks; instead it was mortared in an unusual, asymmetrical and random fashion.

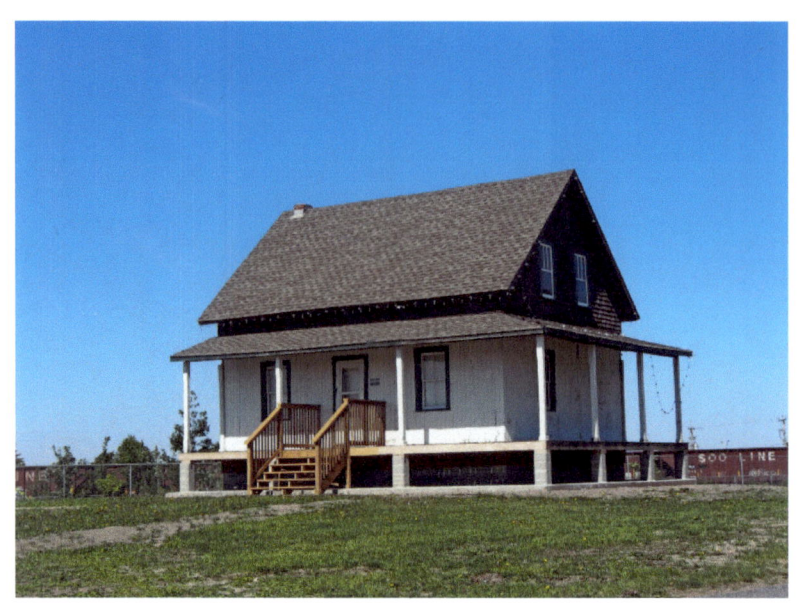

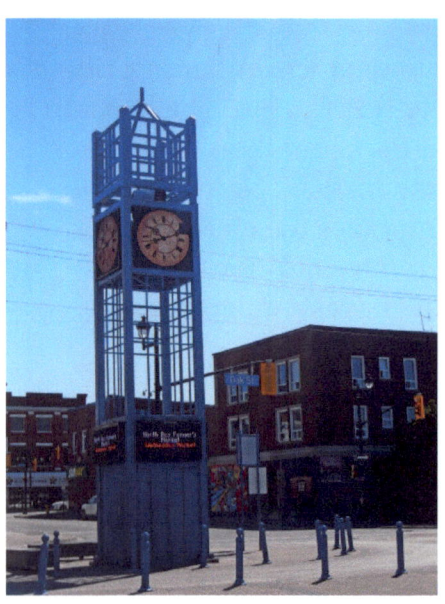
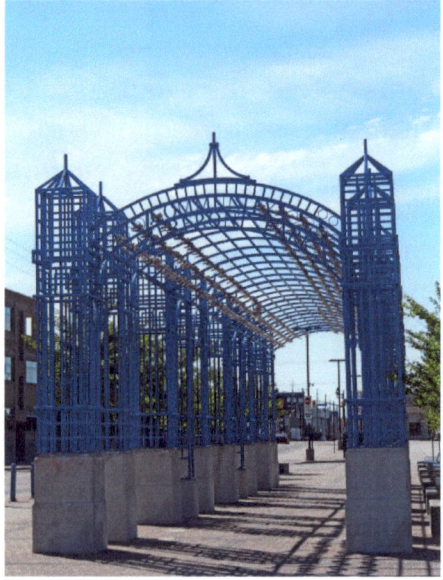

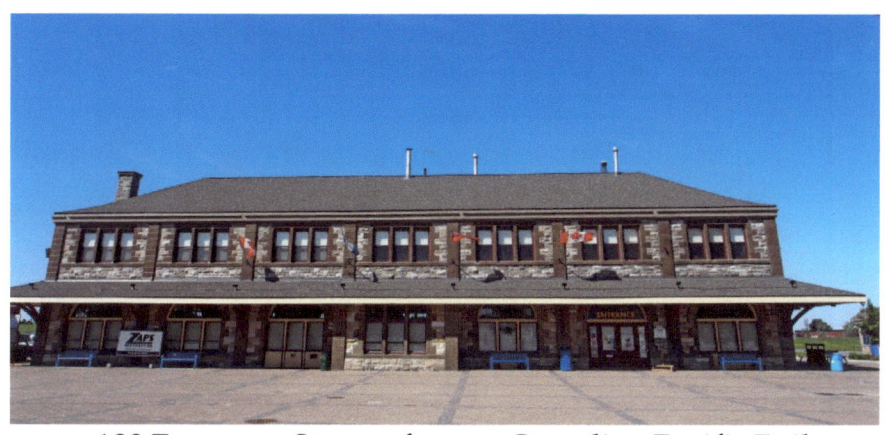

100 Ferguson Street - former Canadian Pacific Railway Station – 1903 - Entry of British Columbia into Confederation in 1871 led to the establishment of the CPR as the initial continental railway linking the country's east and west coasts, completed in 1885. In 1881 the railway located their divisional services and regional headquarters on the shore of Lake Nipissing, where the City of North Bay subsequently sprang up.

The stone masonry is of a variegated light beige color of split-faced finish, laid in a random-coursed pattern. The corner and intermittent piers and window surrounds are of a uniform darker brown tone of flat-faced finish, laid in a level course pattern. Most openings at ground floor level are of the Romanesque round-head arched style. A wide bracketed canopy projects on all sides at the second floor level, offering protection from the weather to passengers, their luggage, and accompanying freight.

The Canadian Pacific Railway reached North Bay in 1882 and the area became a crucial junction point between east and west rail traffic. In 1901, the CPR made North Bay the District Divisional headquarters; repair shops began to dominate the North Bay waterfront.

The site eventually housed an eighteen-stall engine house, freight and flour sheds, carpenter and car repair shops, ice houses, a yard office, railway stores, and the engineer booking office. There was also a vast locomotive shop used to repair steam engines.

At its peak, the yard could hold two hundred railroad cars and it contained twenty-five miles of track. During the 1940s, four transcontinental trains a day came through the yards. To the west of the main depot was a well-maintained grassy park with numerous flower gardens and trees.

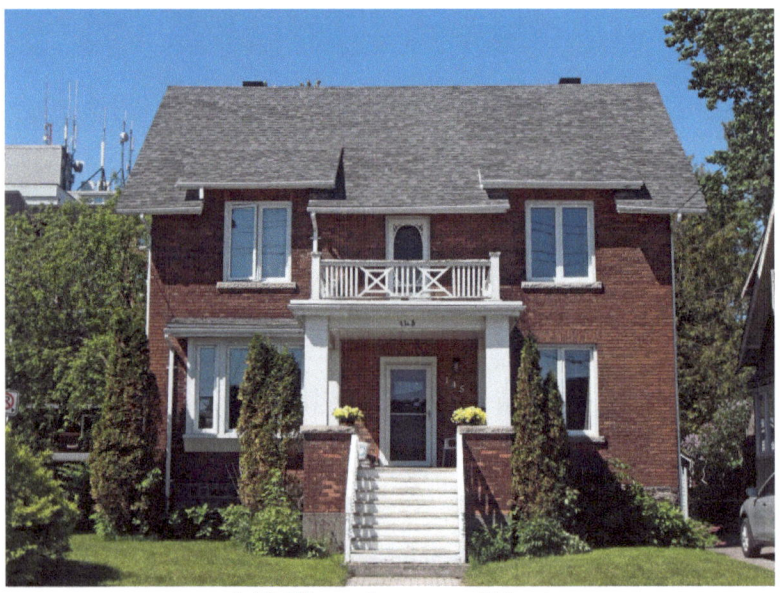

145 First Avenue West

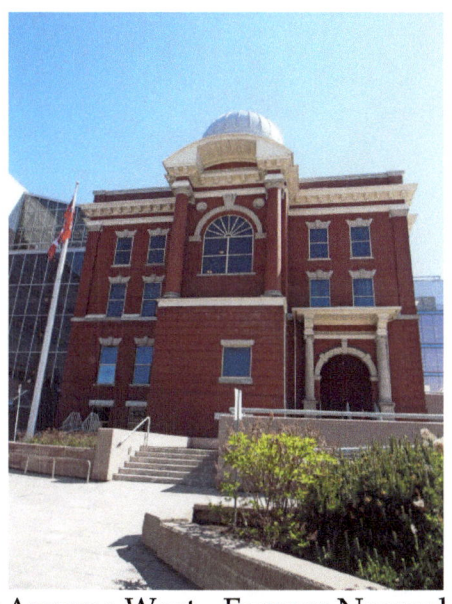

200 First Avenue West - Former Normal School/Teacher's College opened in 1909 with an enrolment of 25 students and continued in operation until 1972. This design is exemplary of the architectural influence of the Edwardian style. The observatory-like dome, the elaborate cornices and the formal entrance are three main characteristics of the building.

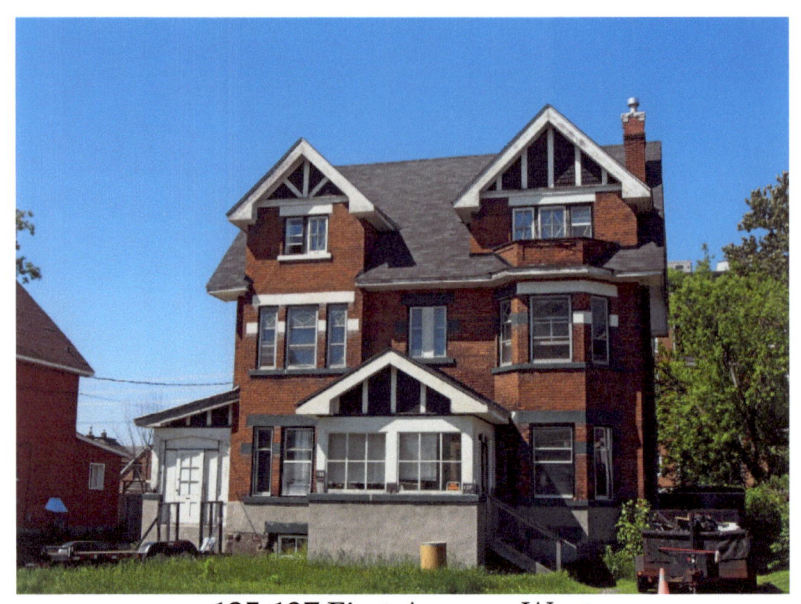

135-137 First Avenue West

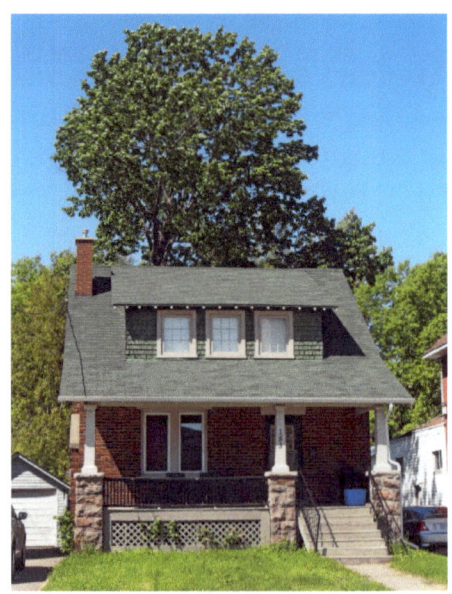

153 First Avenue West

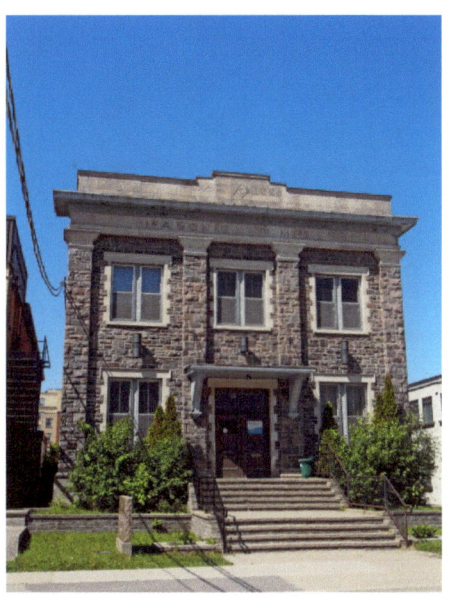

183 First Avenue West - North Bay Masonic Temple was built in 1928 and was first used as a meeting and dance hall. During the Second World War it served as a center for medical examinations of those local residents contemplating military service.

The building is neo-classical in style with a symmetrical front façade. The outstanding architectural features of this building include the engaged piers and stepped parapet carried by the entablature. The grand stone entranceway expresses the major function of this structure as an assembly hall.

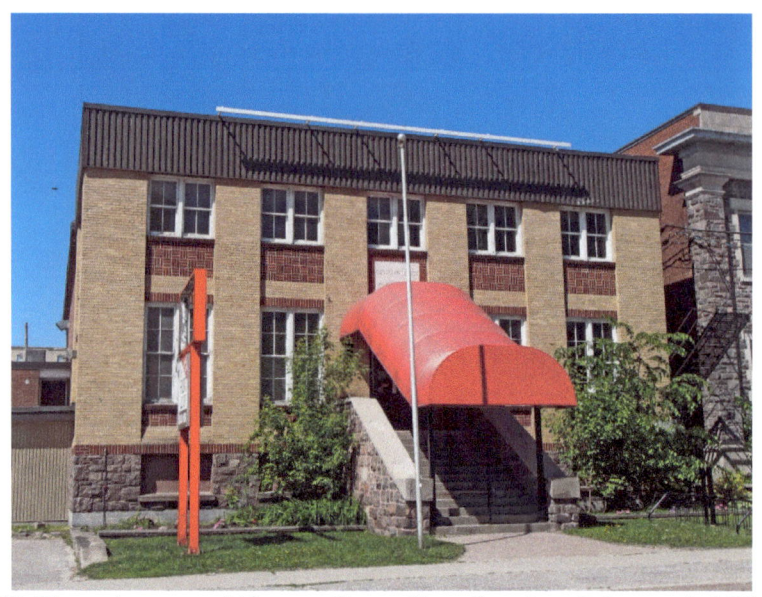

150 First Avenue West – Canadian Legion Memorial Hall

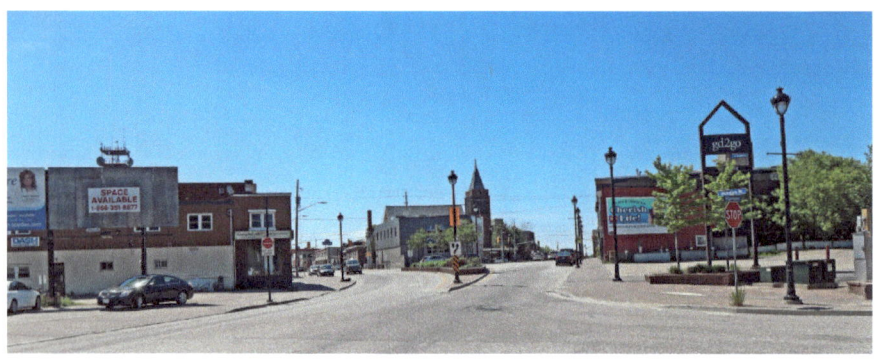

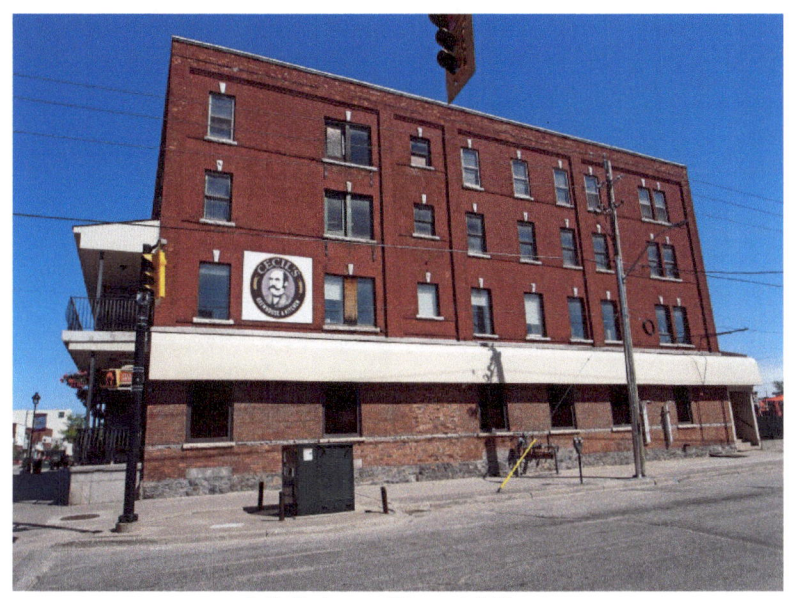

McIntyre Street West

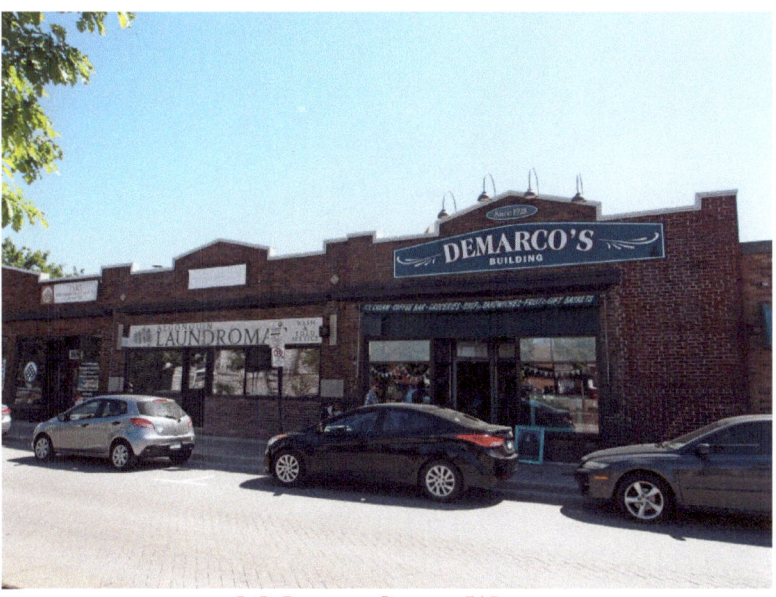

McIntyre Street West

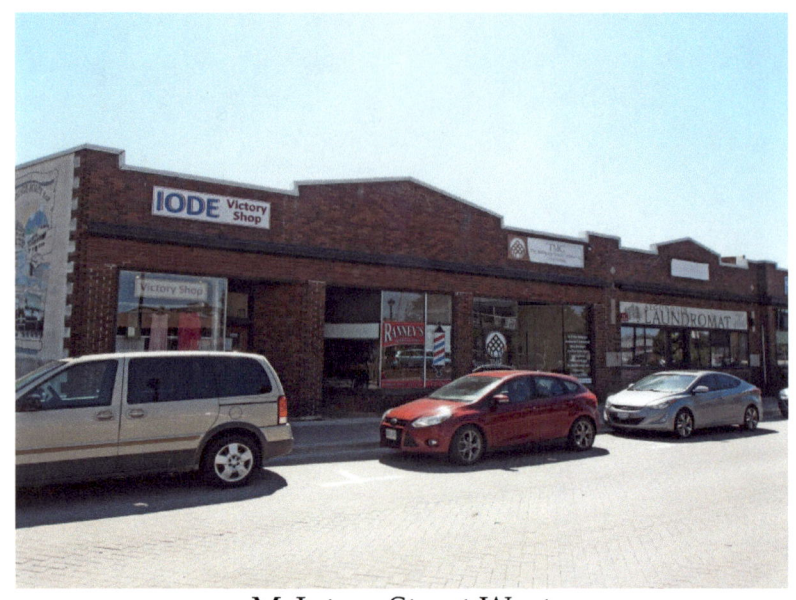

McIntyre Street West

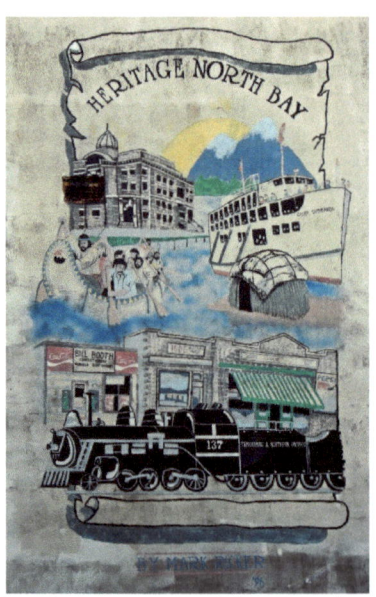

Heritage North Bay Mural by Mark Ricker 1996

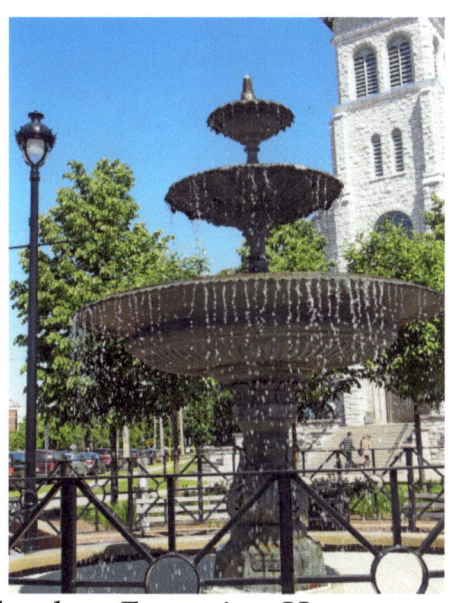

J. W. Richardson Fountain – He was mayor and a horticulturist who devoted much of his life to the betterment and beautification of the city of North Bay.

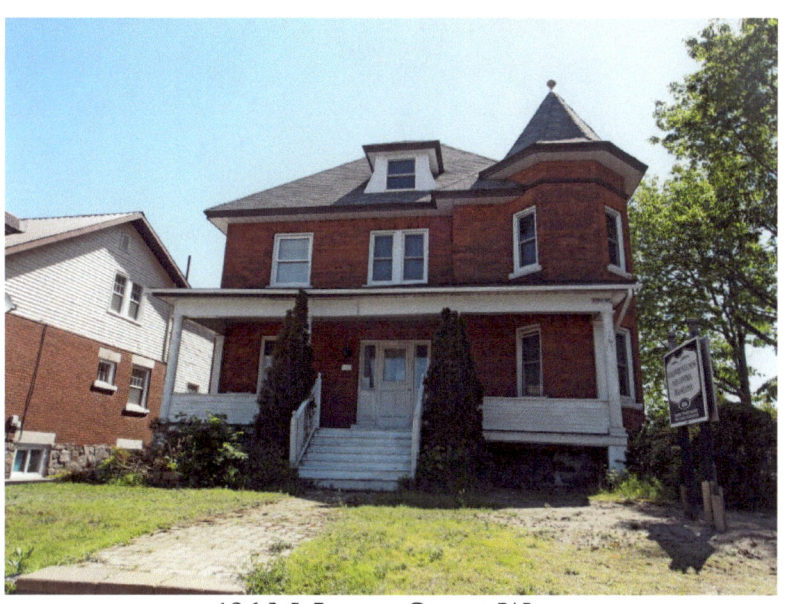

406 McIntyre Street West

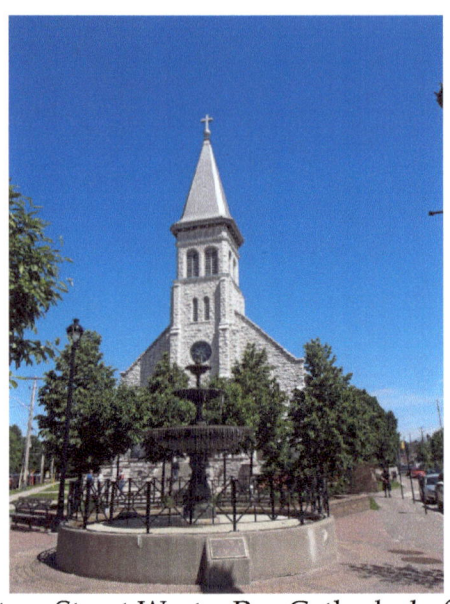

480 McIntyre Street West – Pro-Cathedral of the Assumption – 1904 - The steeple of this white limestone church acts as a beacon in the landscape. Because of the height of the projecting tower, and the open space of the church interior, buttressing of the walls was needed for structural stability.

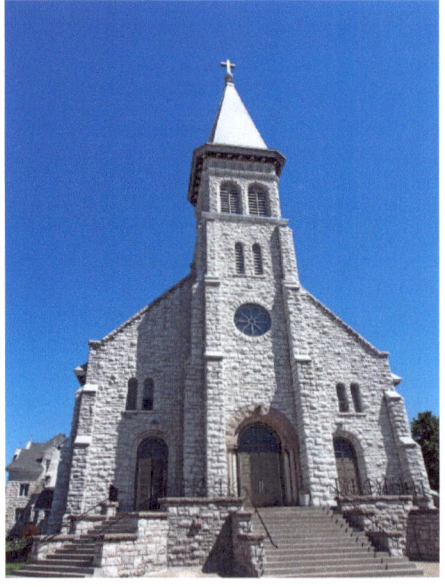

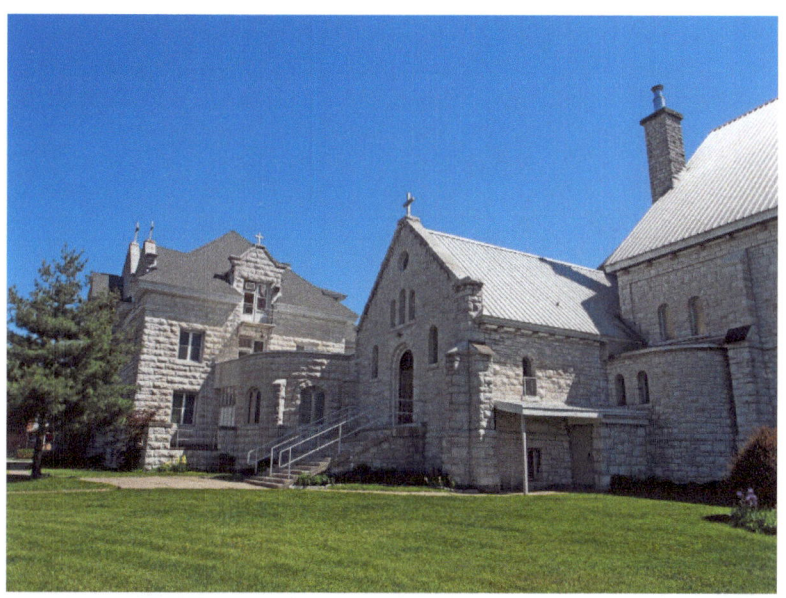

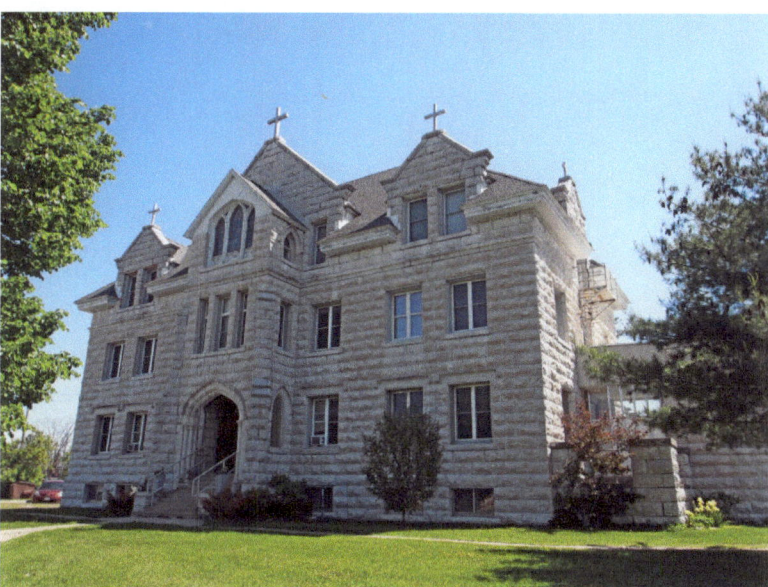

In 1911, the rectory was built using the same material and architectural forms as those of the church thus blending the two structures into one form. This addition became known as "The Bishop's Palace."

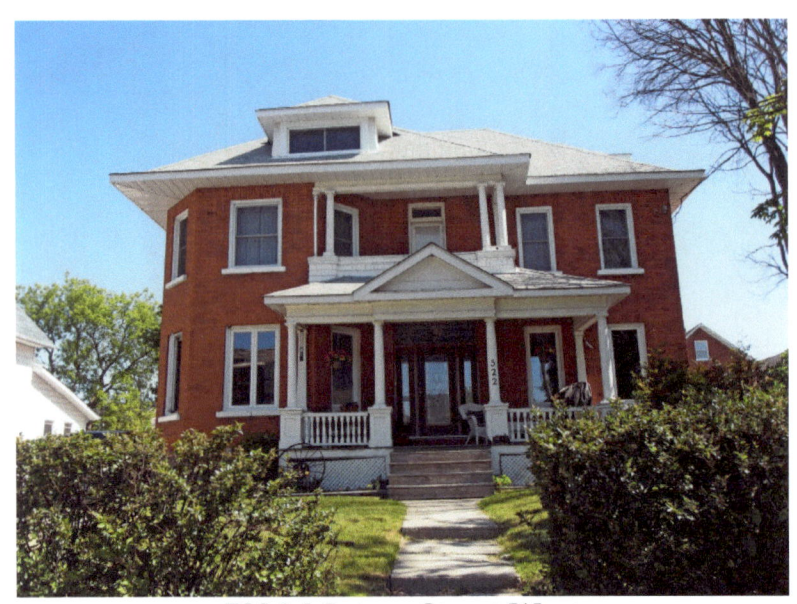

522 McIntyre Street West

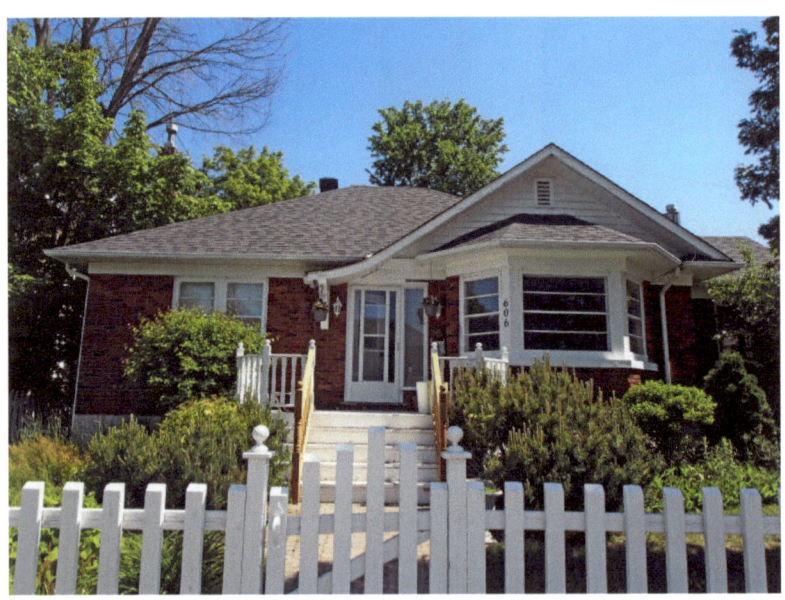

606 McIntyre Street West

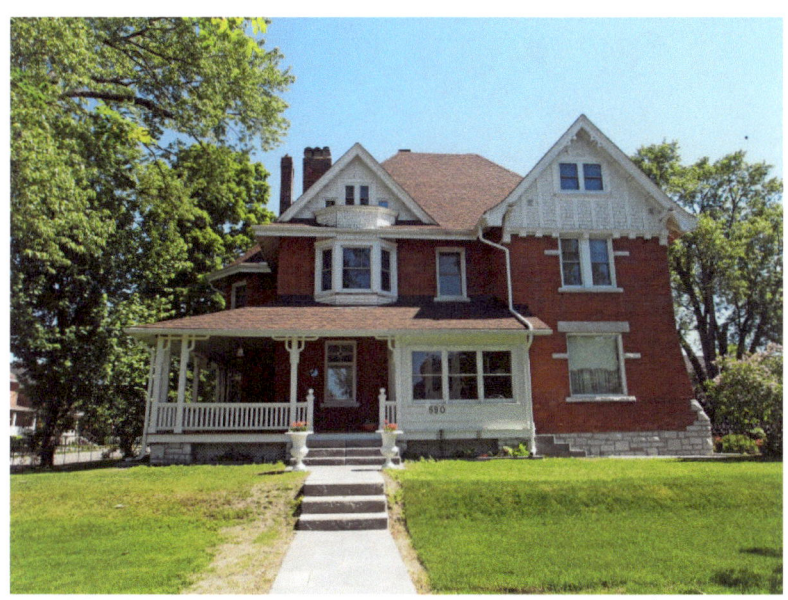

590 McIntyre Street West - Browning Residence - Constructed in 1902, it was originally occupied by Crown Prosecutor A.G. Browning and his family. It is set on a large corner lot at Murray Street, among mature trees.

     A strong symmetry of the main façade was originally developed in a 3 bay roofed front porch at ground floor level leading to the main entry, above which is a second floor bay window whose structure extends through the main roof eave to form a unique mini-balcony centered on a third floor windowed gable. This symmetry is offset by a three story gabled wing on one side, and the wrap-around porch terminating at a corner bay on the Murray Street side.

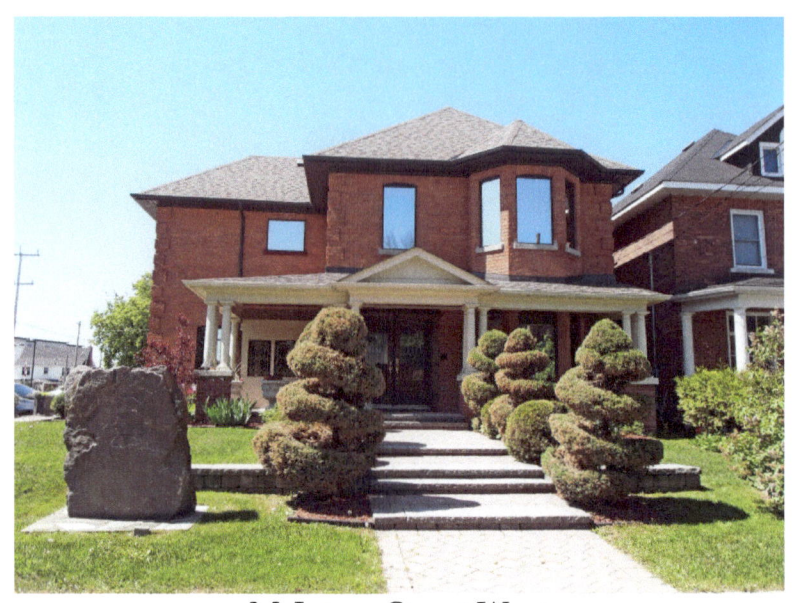

McIntyre Street West

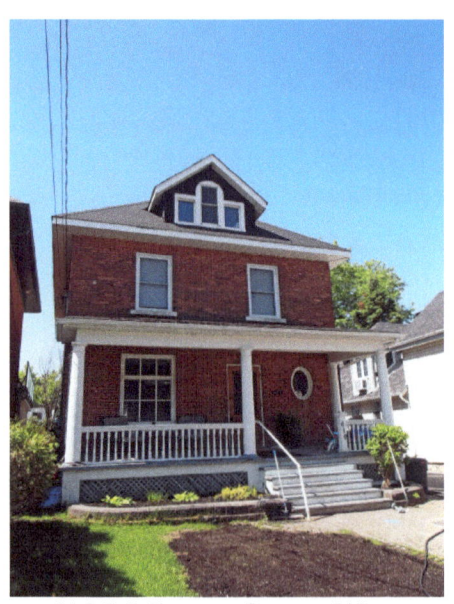

619 McIntyre Street West

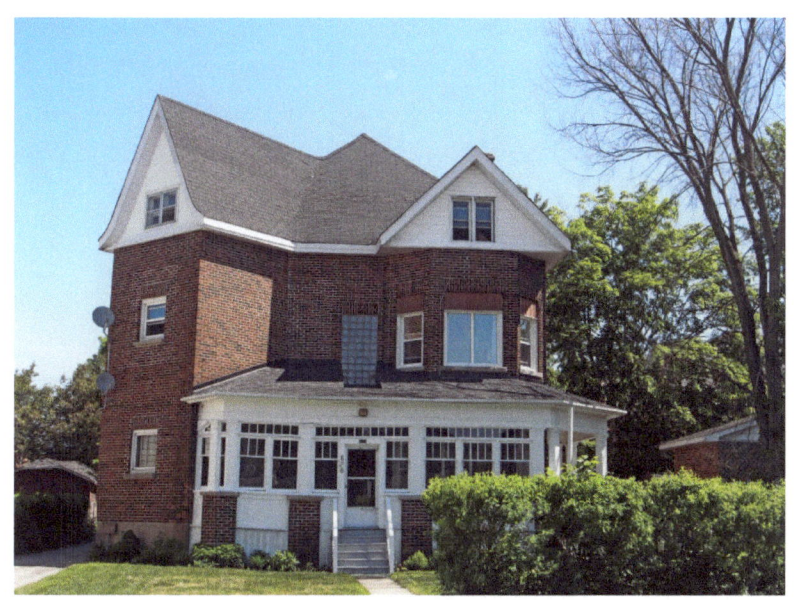

620 McIntyre Street West

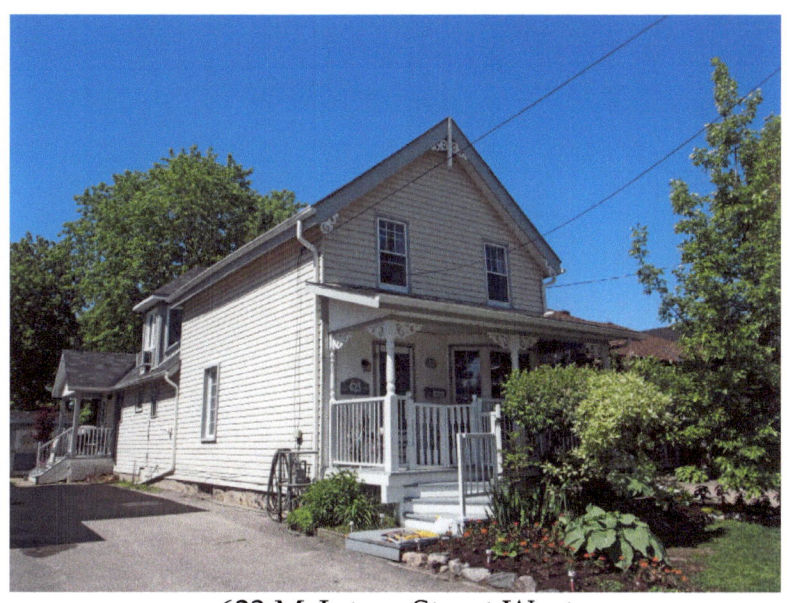

623 McIntyre Street West

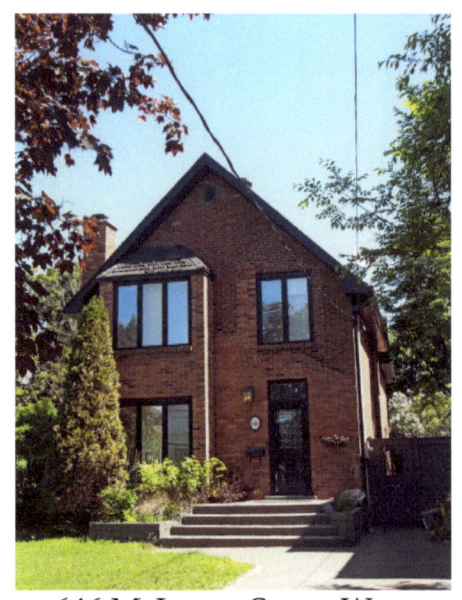

646 McIntyre Street West

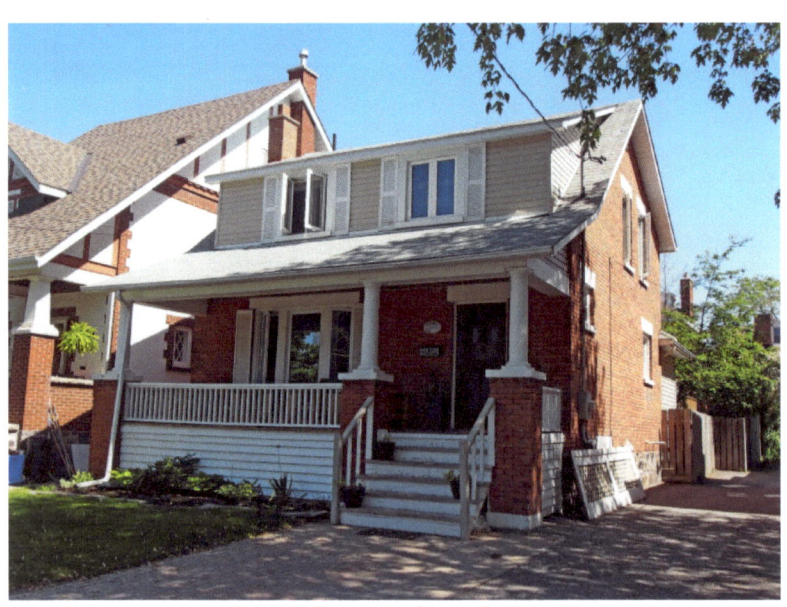

686 McIntyre Street West

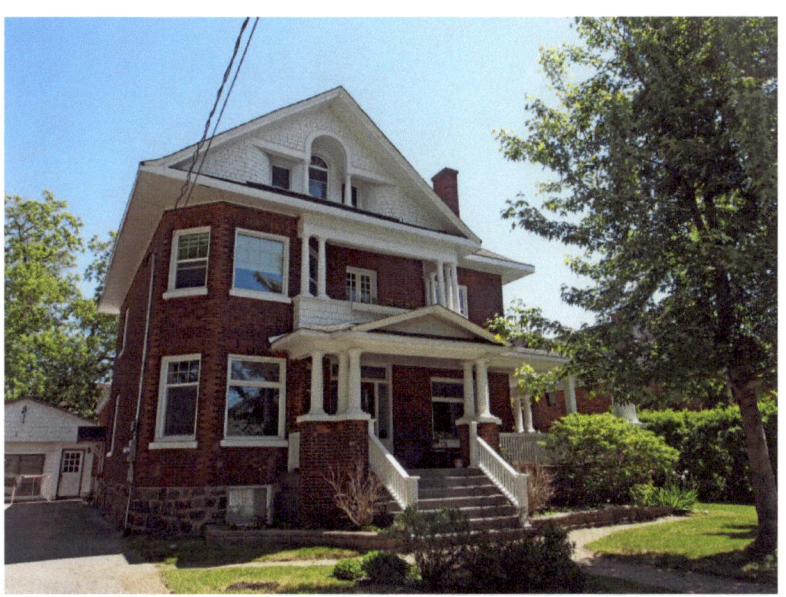

658 McIntyre Street West – The Bourke Residence was built in 1907. The structural, yet decorative columns and the boxed-in triangular pediment over the porch area are strong elements of the design. The two story bay windows and the wraparound porch are also distinctive. Symmetry is established, centered on the main entrance, in the access stair, the pediment enhanced porch, and the second floor balcony. The windowed gable at the attic level is centered independently on the main front wing of the L-shaped structure.

The home was once the residence of the first Mayor of the City of North Bay, John Bourke.

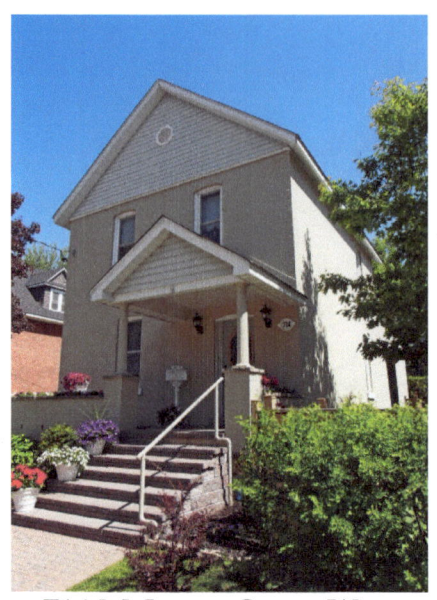

714 McIntyre Street West

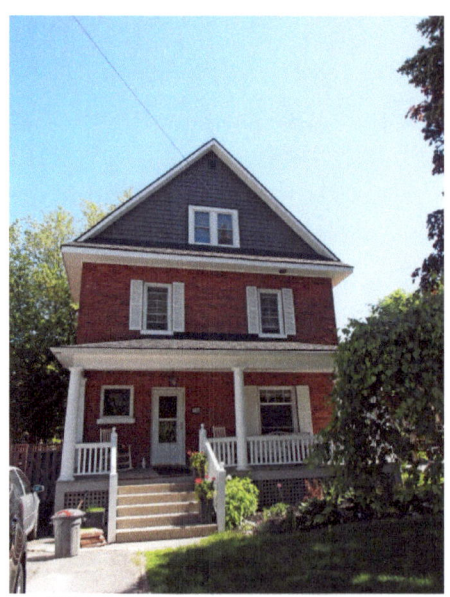

732 McIntyre Street West

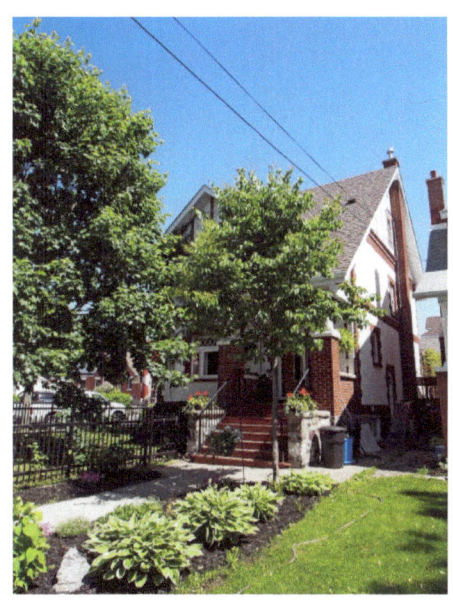

McIntyre Street West

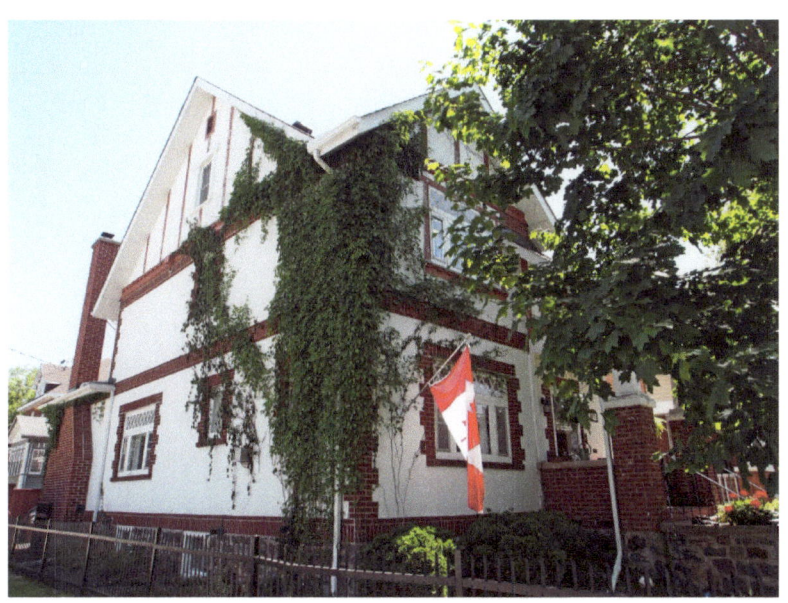

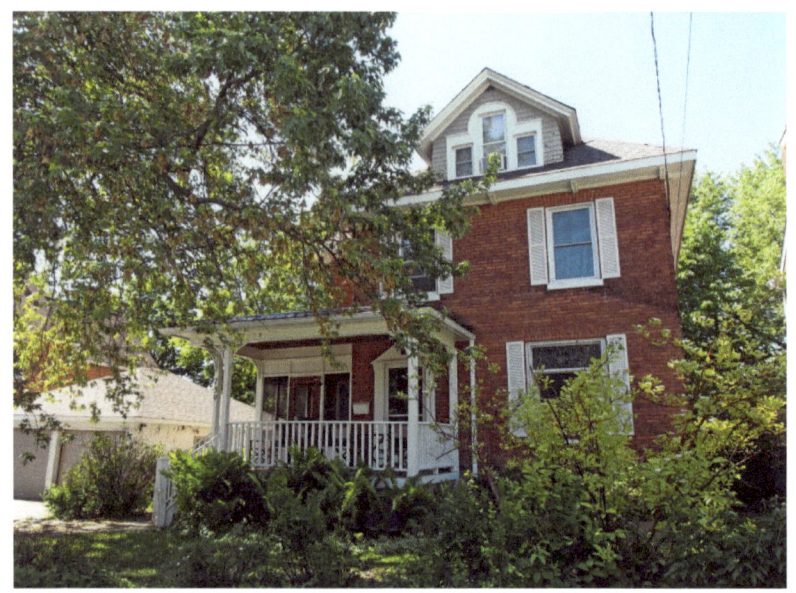

739 McIntyre Street West

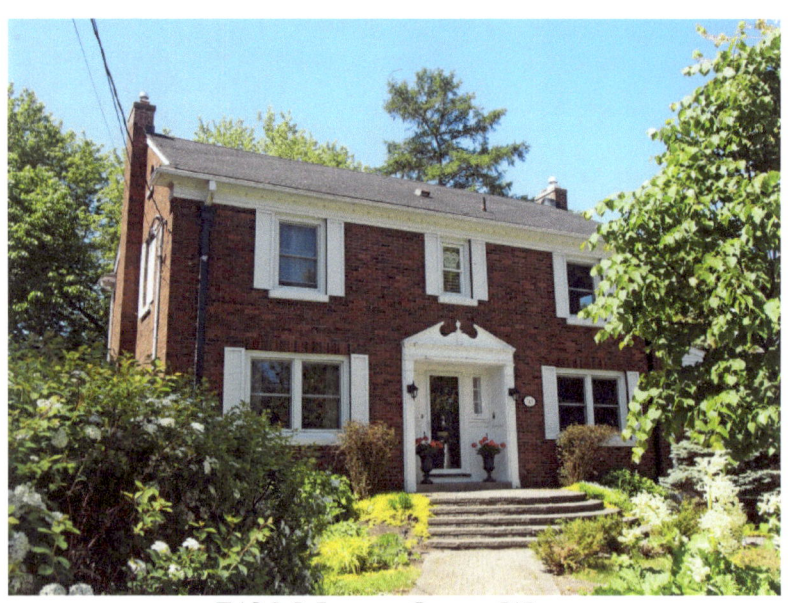

749 McIntyre Street West

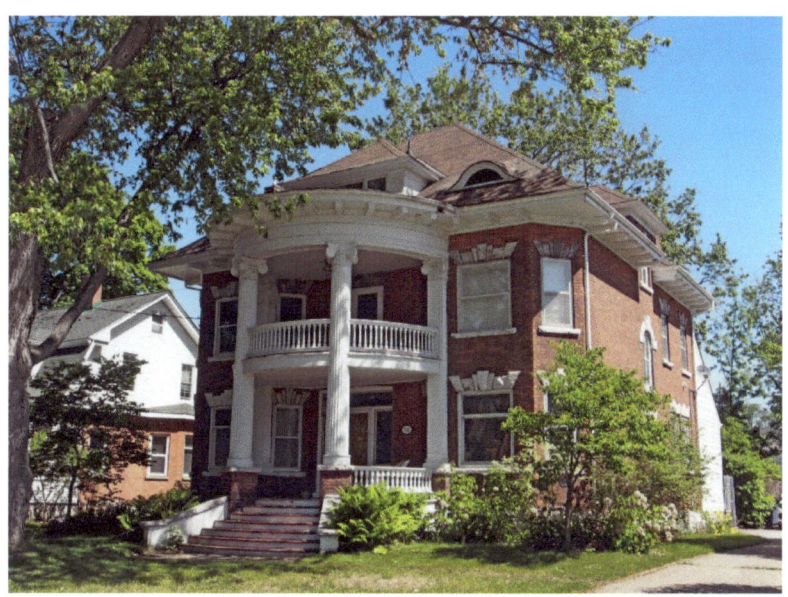

    768 McIntyre Street West – The Beamish Residence was constructed in 1907. The two story front porch is large and has Ionic columns. It has a hipped roof with wave-form dormer windows. A strong symmetry is centered on the two-story wood porch between matched masonry bays. The fanned steps of the main entry are very generous in scale, and thus appropriately related to the proportions of the entire front façade. The front entrance is the only item that is off center.

    A well preserved home of majestic stature, it was once the original residence of a local merchant, Mr. Beamish. Mr. Jack Shaw, former North Bay Mayor, also resided here. Mr. Arthur Cavanaugh, former manager of Ontario Northland Railway, lived in this house from 1940-1950.

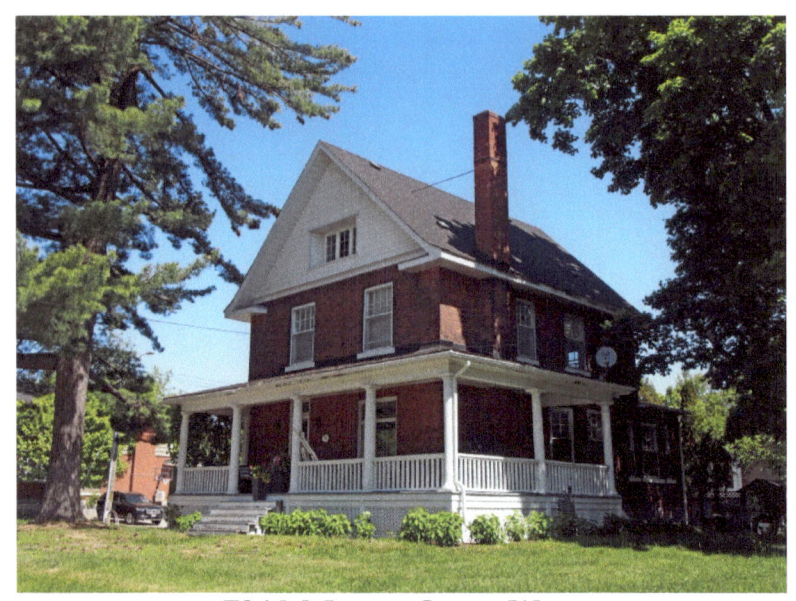

796 McIntyre Street West

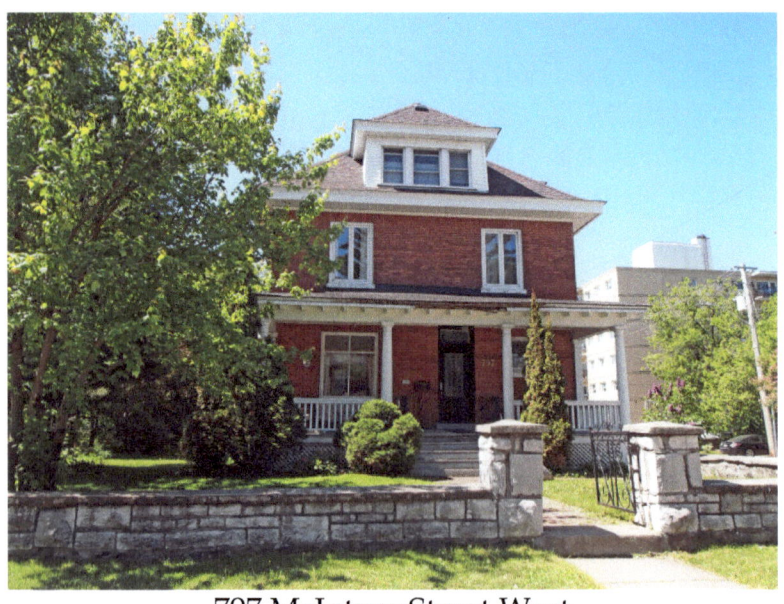

797 McIntyre Street West

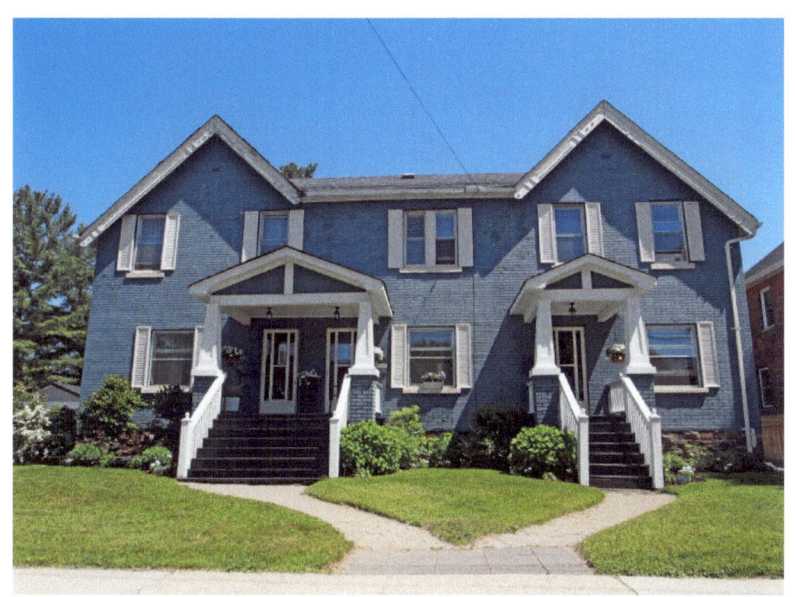

552-542 McIntyre Street West

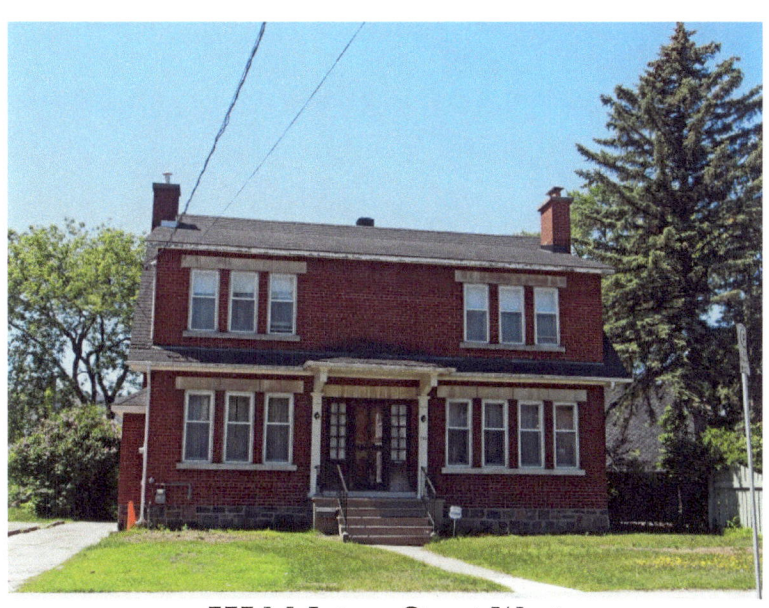

555 McIntyre Street West

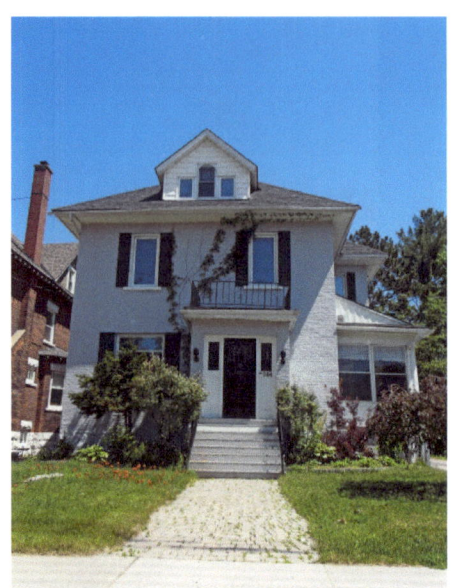

564 McIntyre Street West

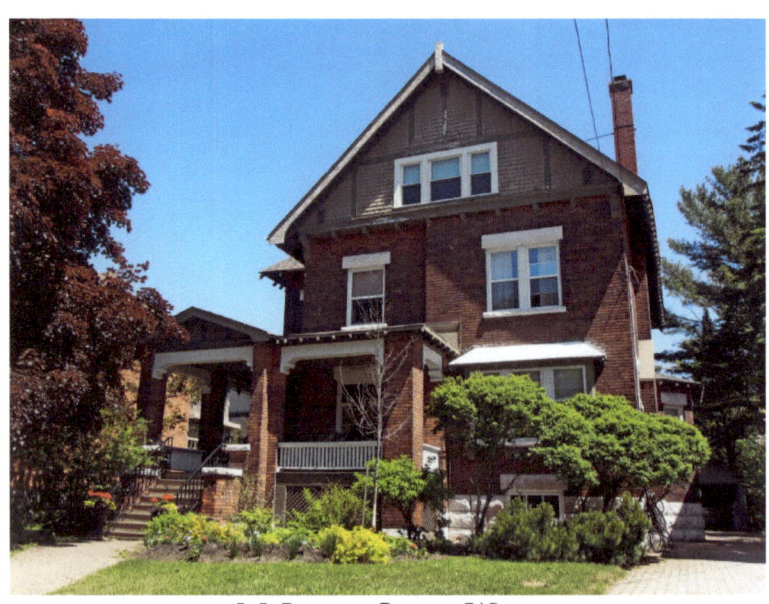

McIntyre Street West

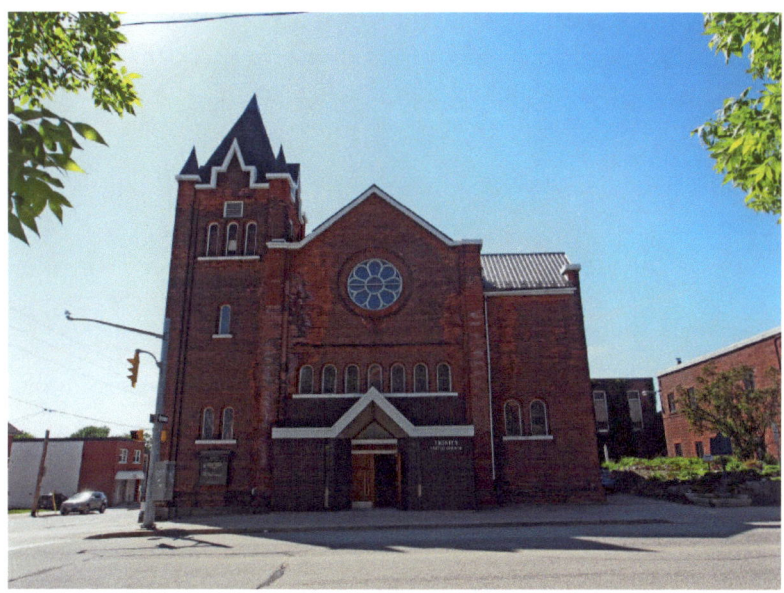

111 McIntyre Street East - Trinity United Church employs a mixture of forms borrowed from both Romanesque and Gothic styles in window arrangements. It was constructed in 1906. The end gable rose window, the large side tower and clerestory windows are some of the key features of this design.

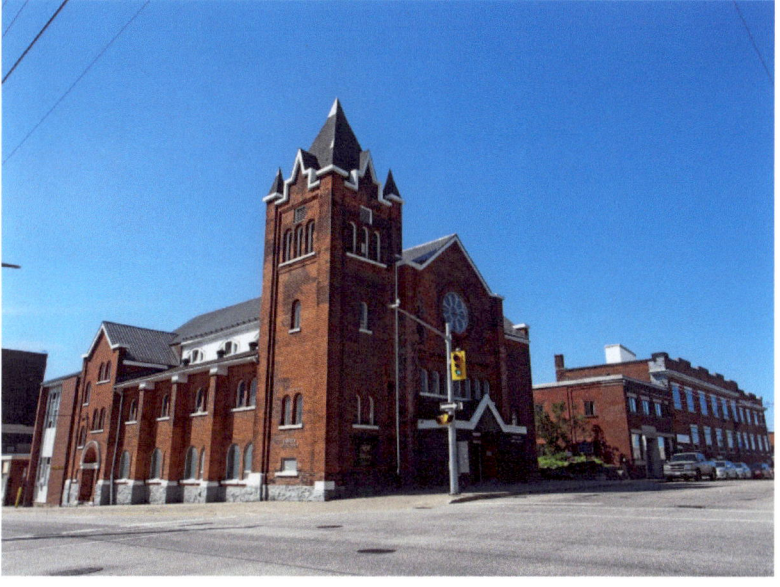

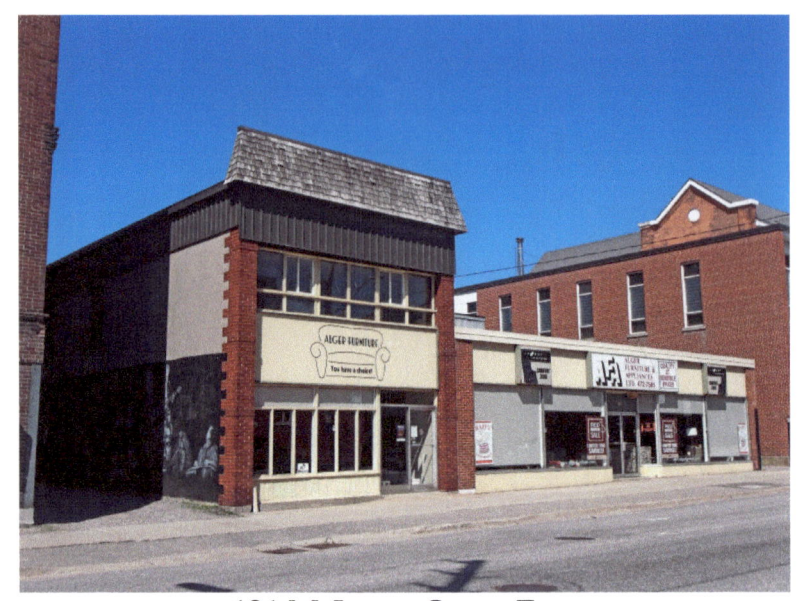

131 McIntyre Street East

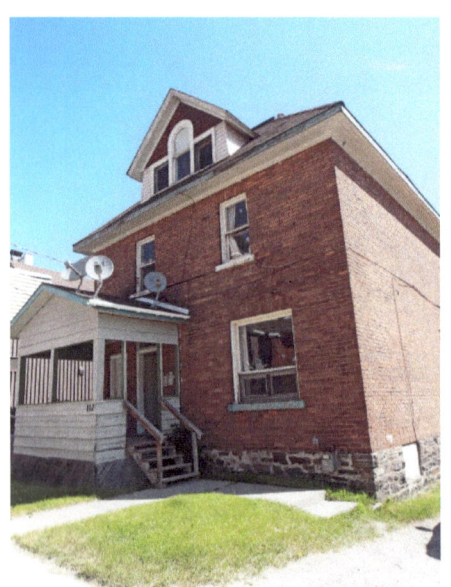

112 McIntyre Street East

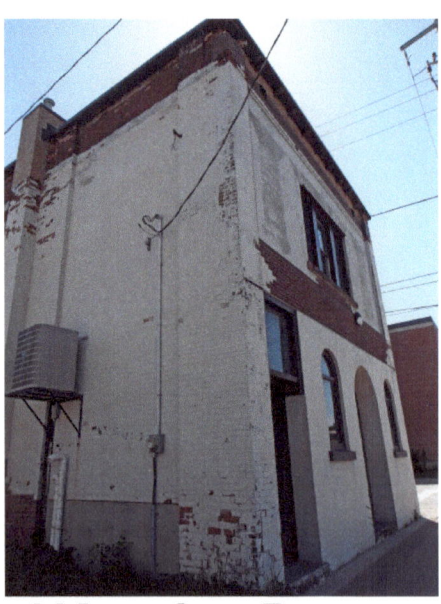

McIntyre Street East

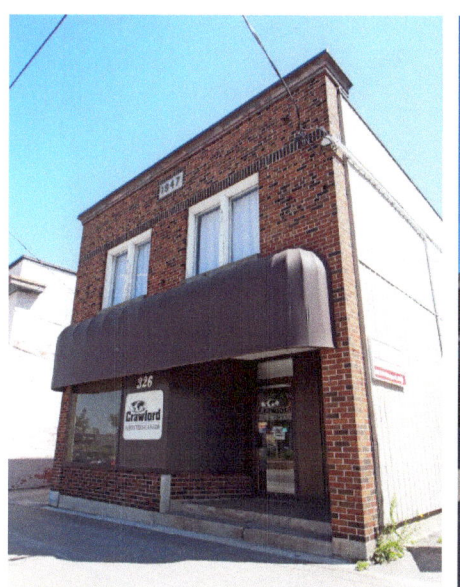
326 McIntyre Street East

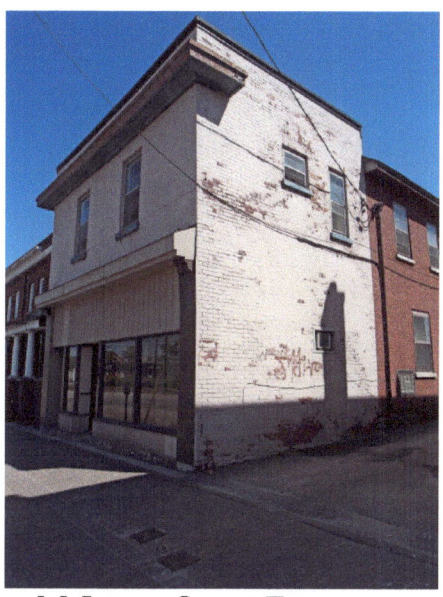
McIntyre Street East

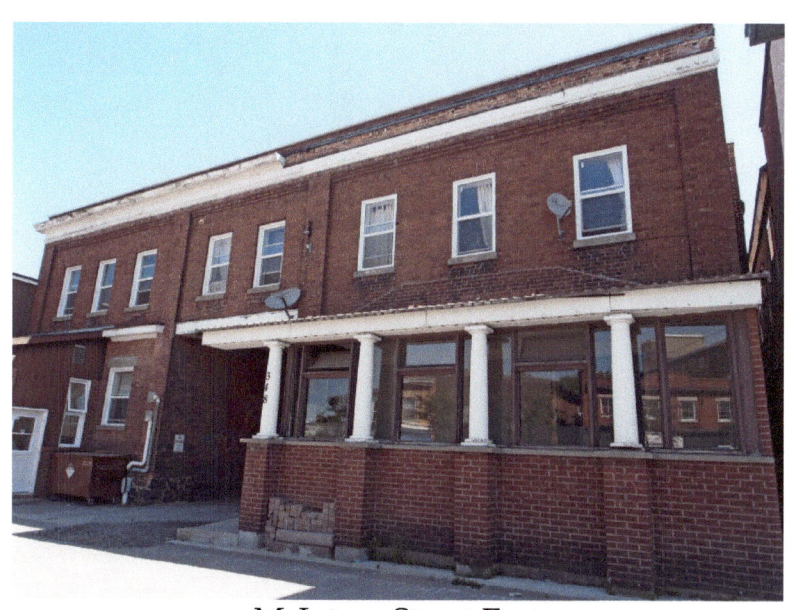
McIntyre Street East

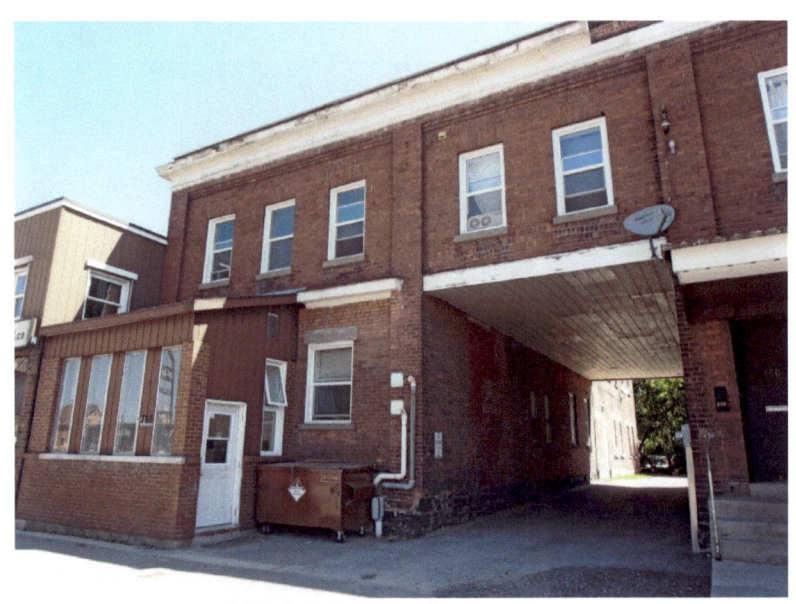

350 McIntyre Street East

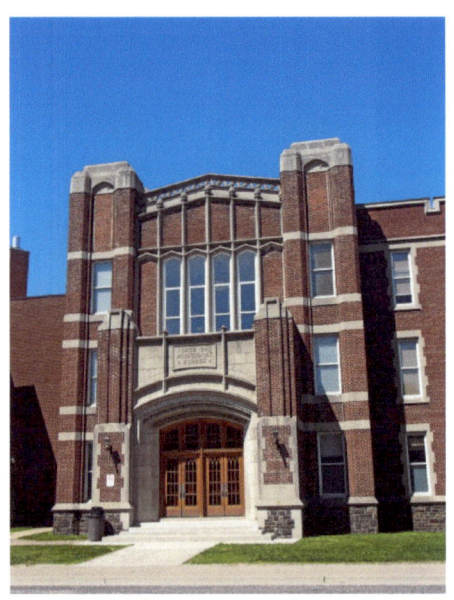

555 Algonquin Avenue

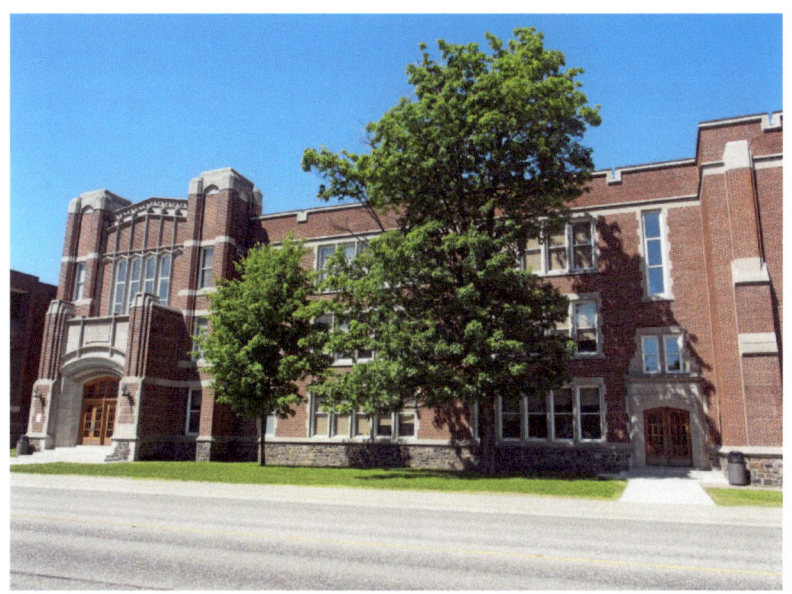

555 Algonquin Avenue - Former North Bay Collegiate Institute & Vocational School – 1930 - The building has a projecting frontispiece with a recessed entrance with heavy oak doors. A secondary entrance has the motto "Learn to Live" inscribed in stone above the door.

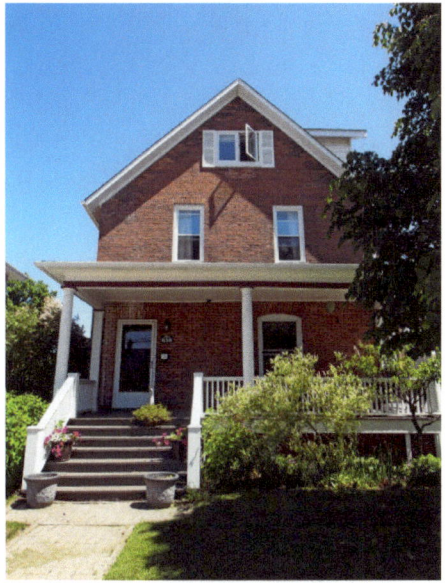

638 Copeland Avenue

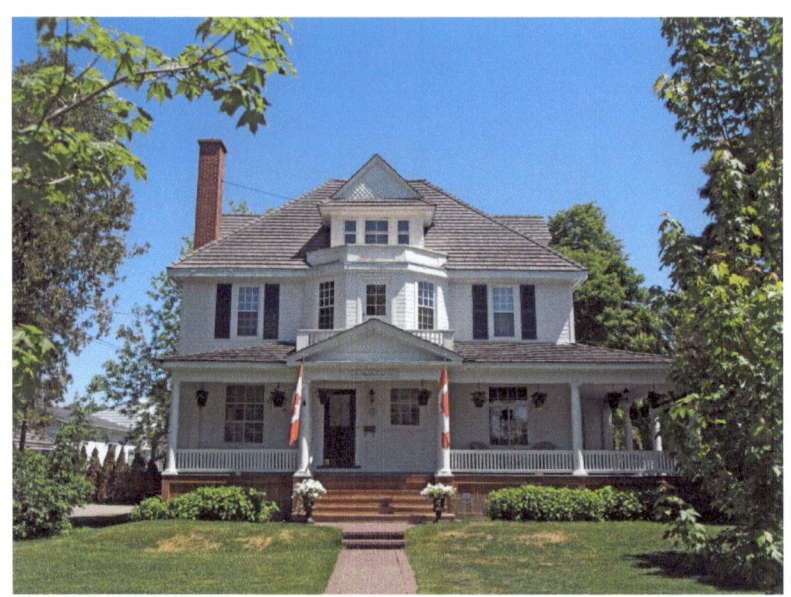

610 Copeland Avenue – The Milne Residence is an impressive home located on an unusually large lot. It was built for William Milne Sr. in the early 1900s. Milne was the owner of Wm. Milne & Sons Lumber Company which was located at the present site of the Ministry of Natural Resources on Trout Lake Road from the early 1900s to 1944. Milne was also a former alderman and Mayor of North Bay in 1909 and 1910.

The house is set back on the property. The large side yard housed a tennis court during the first two decades of the house. The exterior is simple, but the structure is reminiscent of the local history of the lumber and crafts industry. The exterior walls are sheathed with shiplap-type wood siding. The roof is sheathed in wood shingles. The veranda, which wraps around the front and side of the home, once extended to the rear of the home as well, but it was later removed.

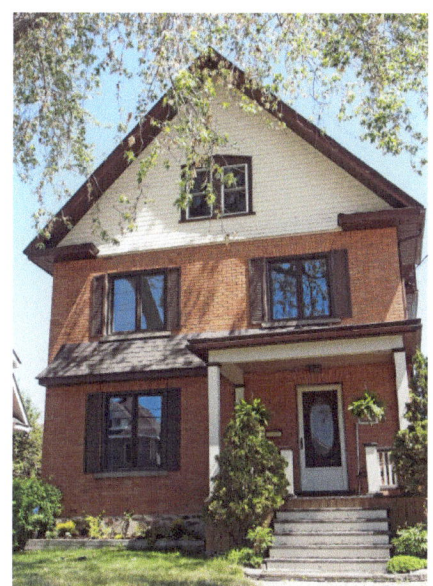

Copeland Avenue

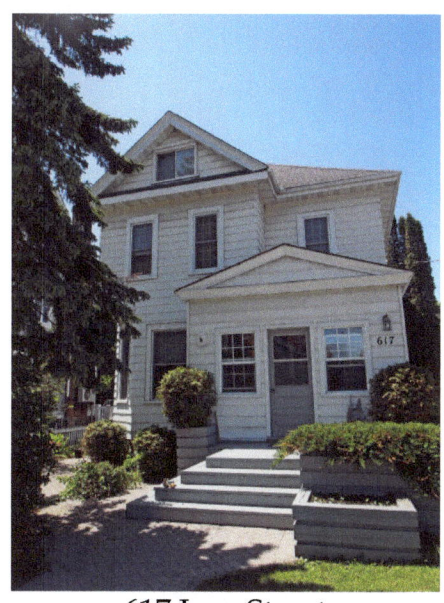

617 Jane Street

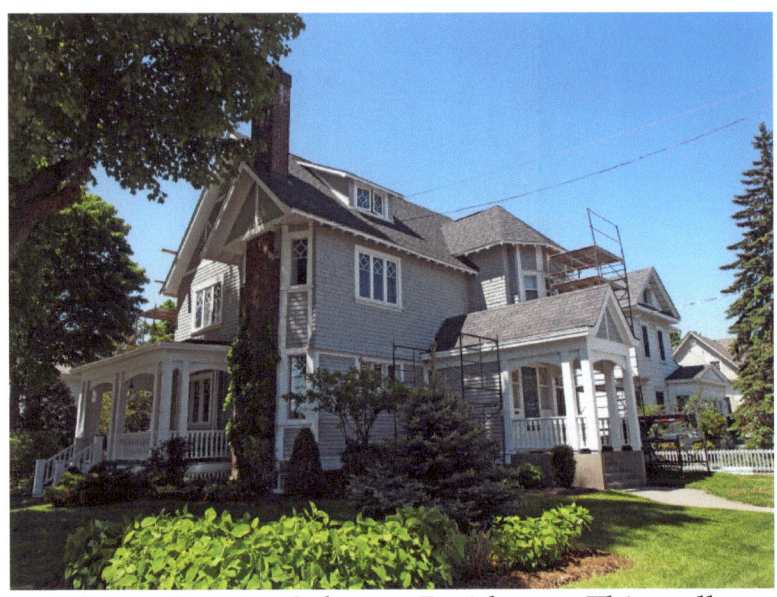

607 Jane Street – Coleman Residence - This well-preserved private home is located in an older, prestigious residential neighborhood, directly across the street from the former North Bay Collegiate Institute and Vocational School. The house was constructed in 1910-11 by Charles Coleman, of Coleman and Prest, local coal dealers. Mrs. Coleman was a daughter of William Milne Sr. and brother to Colonel William Milne, all of the Milne Lumber Company.

The house has diamond shaped upper panes in the restored windows. A generous rear porch is an integral component of this design, affording both visual and physical access to the beautiful landscaped gardens.

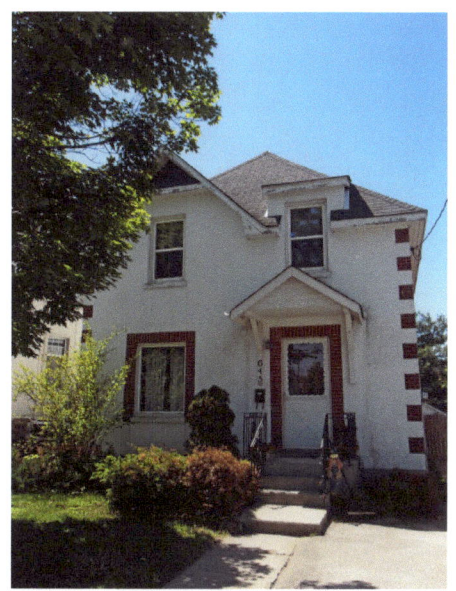

645 Jane Street

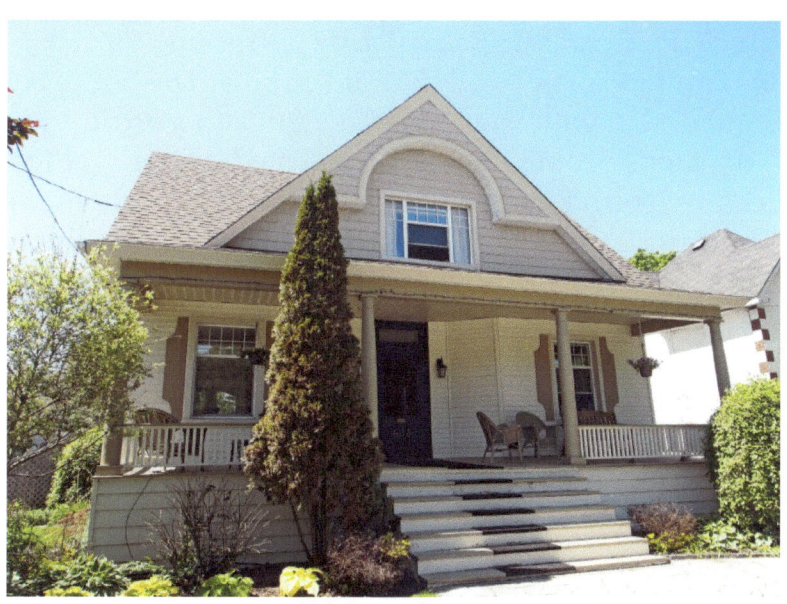

633 Jane Street

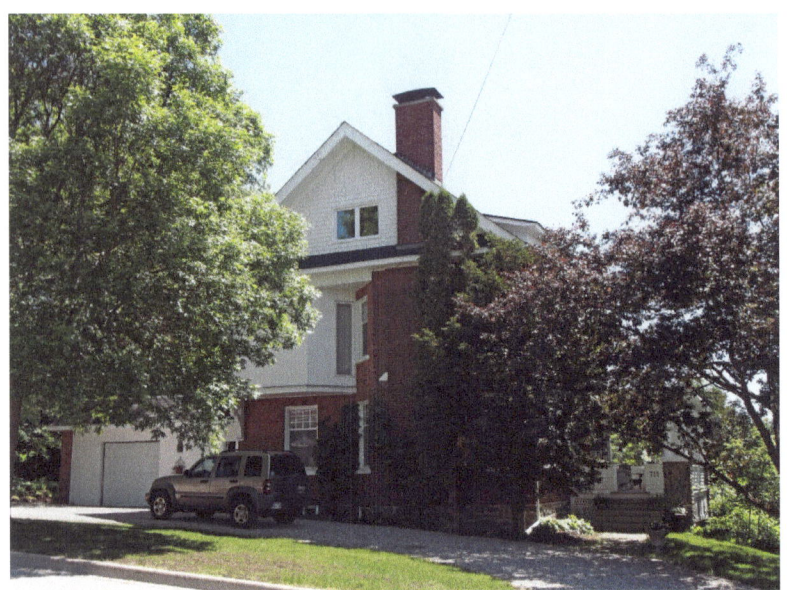

715 Durril Street - The McNutt Residence was built in 1915 for Beatrice Maude Parmelee by Jeffrey and Stevens, notable contractors in North Bay at the time. The house has a rectangular plan with wood construction and a brick veneer.

It stands prominently at an elevated height over the west end of North Bay and over Lake Nipissing. Although the street address is on Durril Street, the street façade is actually the side of the house, with the front of the home facing the lake. The design of the interior has also taken the lake view into account, with the orientation of the principal spaces, including the living room, dining room and master suite, designed to frame the panoramic view from the hilltop location.

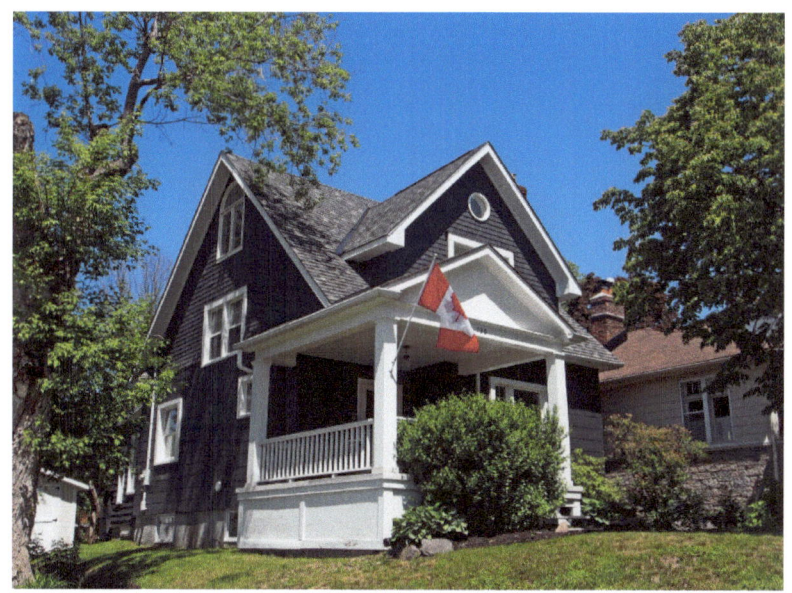

720 Durril Street

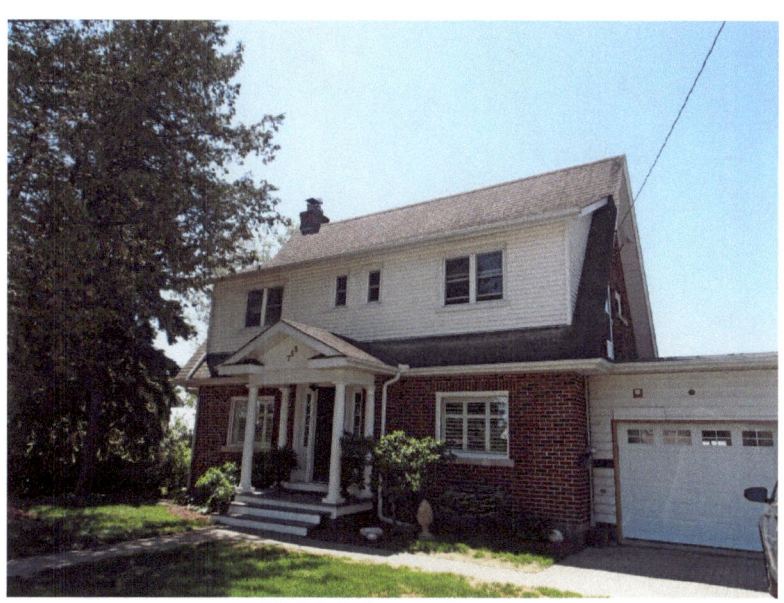

753 Mclaren Street

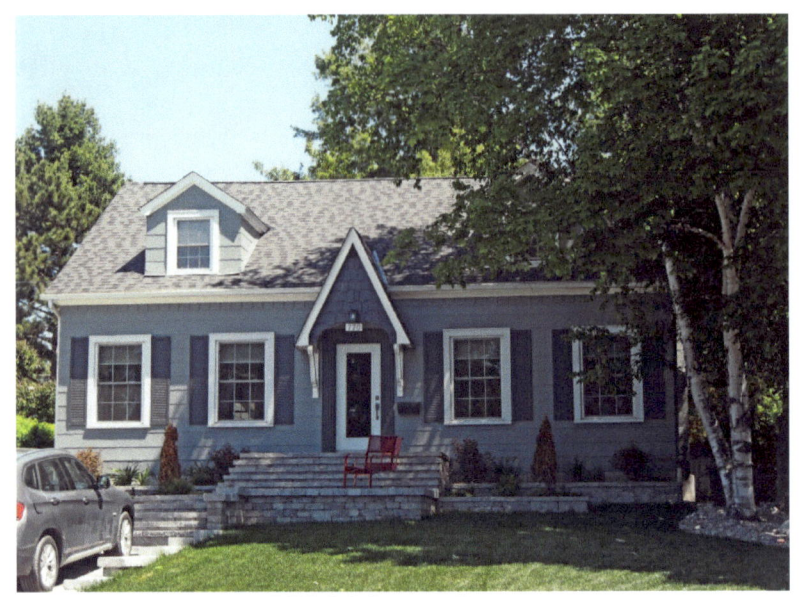
770 Mclaren Street

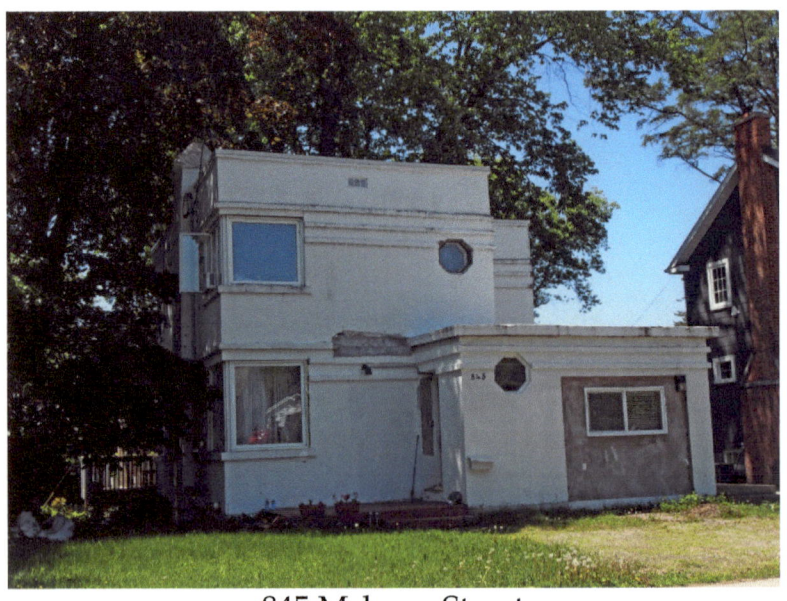
845 Mclaren Street

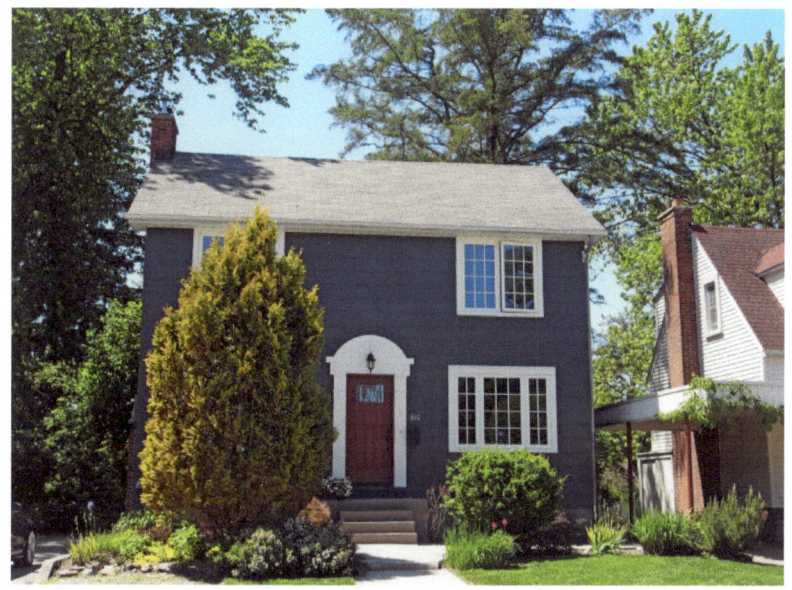

865 Mclaren Street

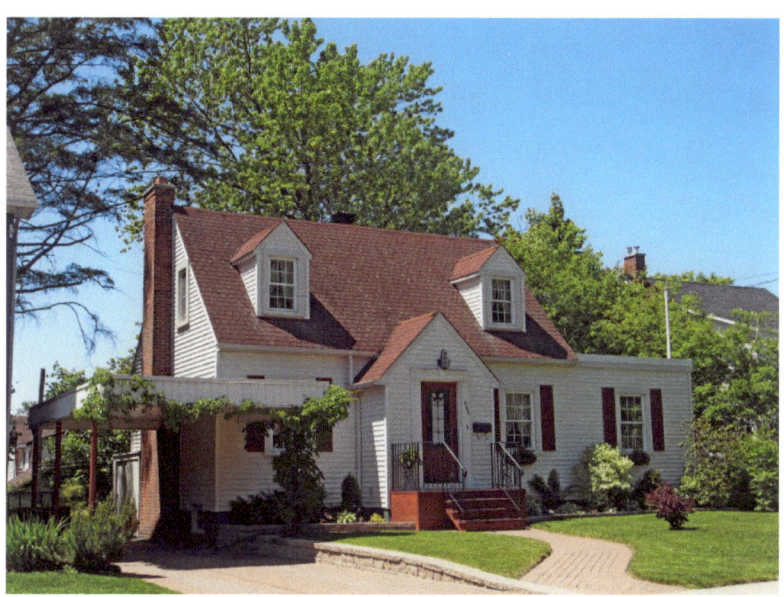

889 Mclaren Street

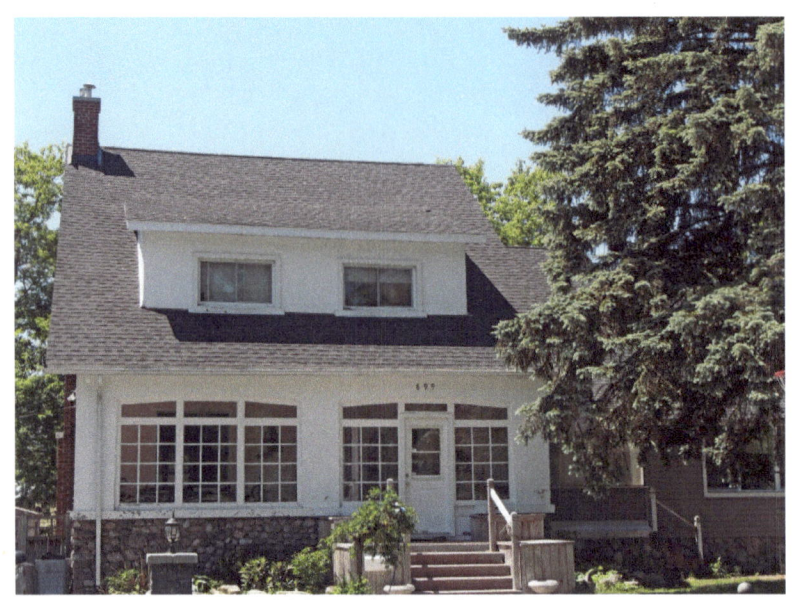

899 Mclaren Street

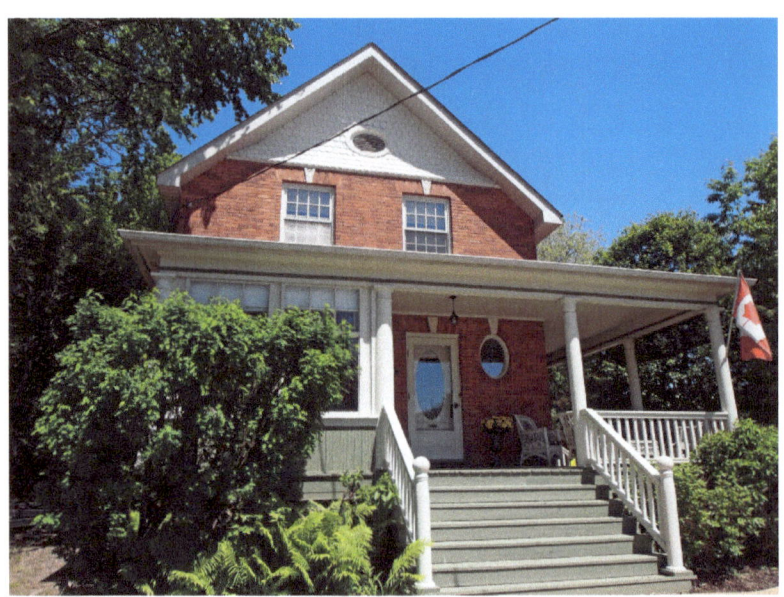

774 Bloem Street

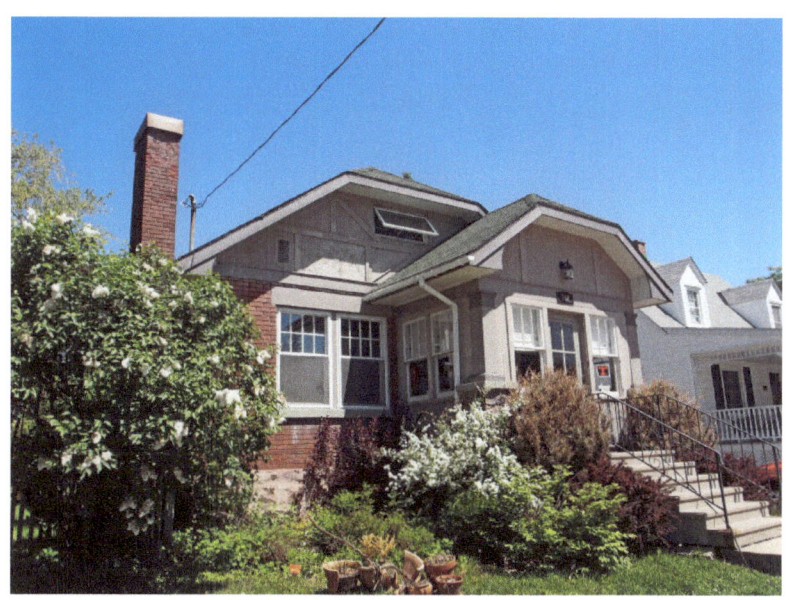
752 Bloem Street

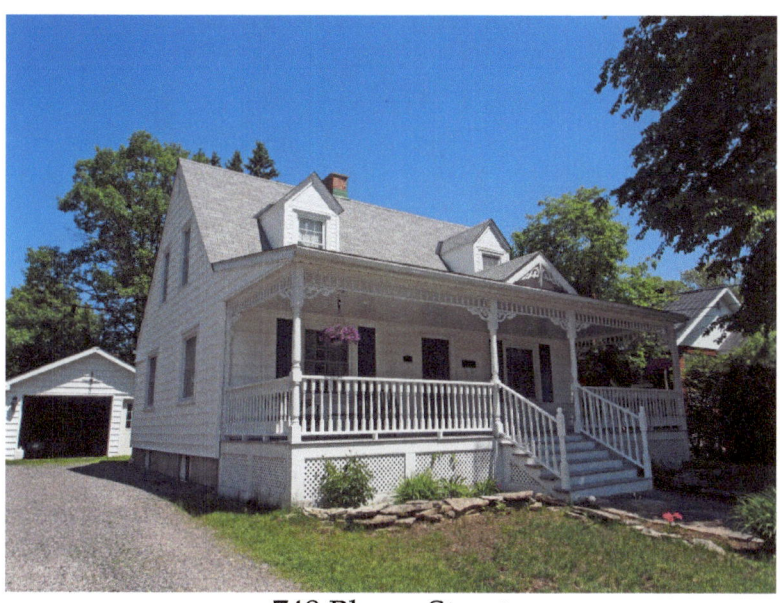
748 Bloem Street

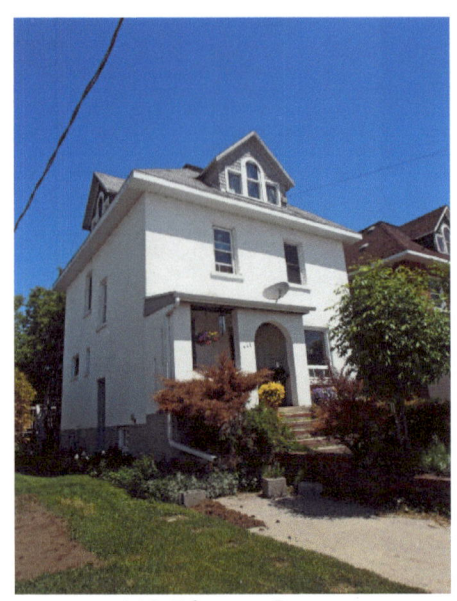

662 Bloem Street

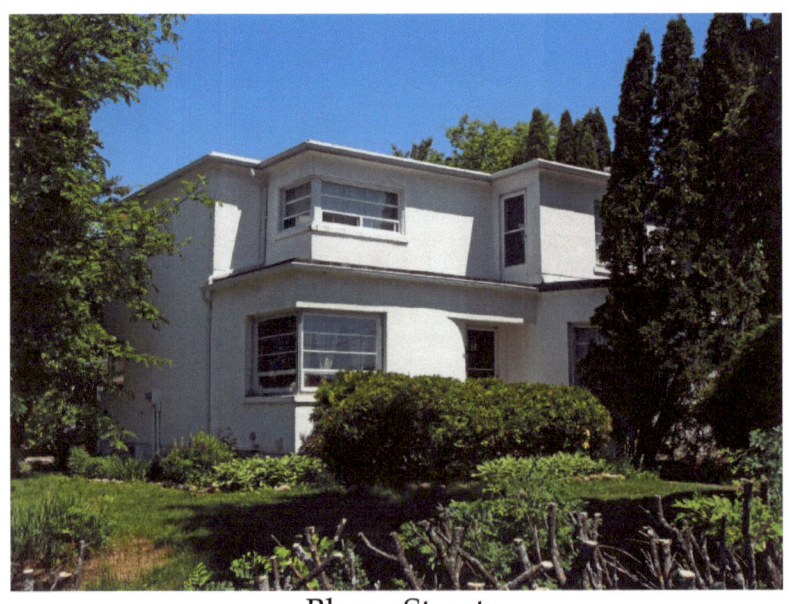

Bloem Street

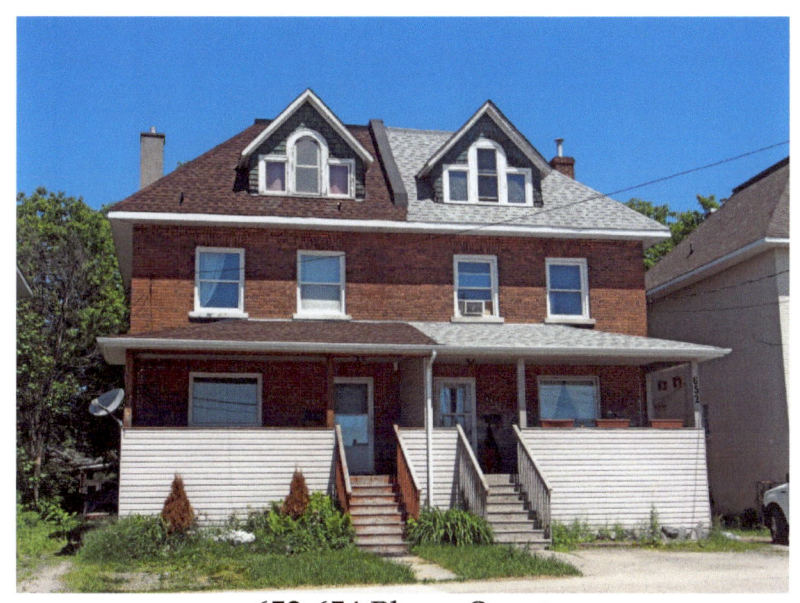

652-654 Bloem Street

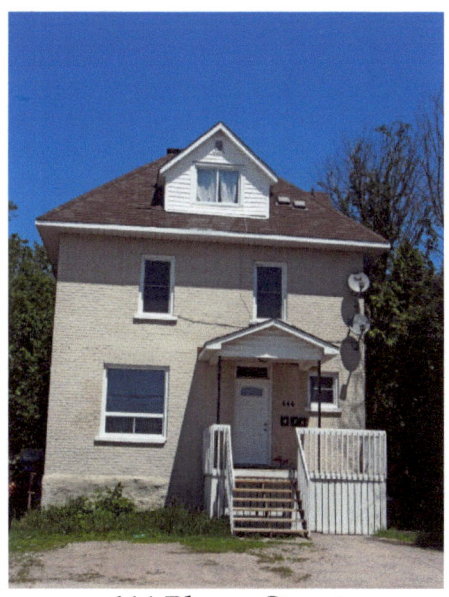

644 Bloem Street

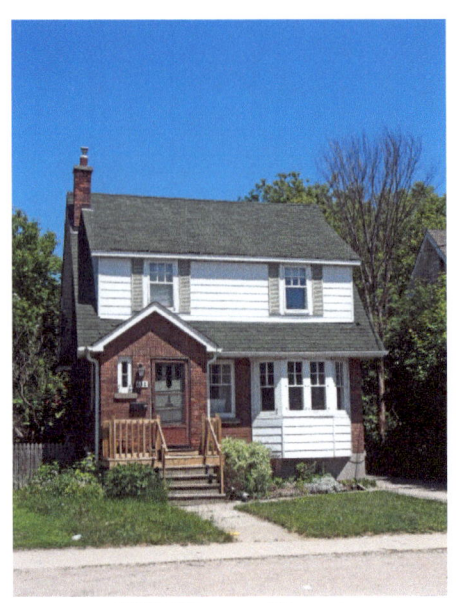

632 Bloem Street

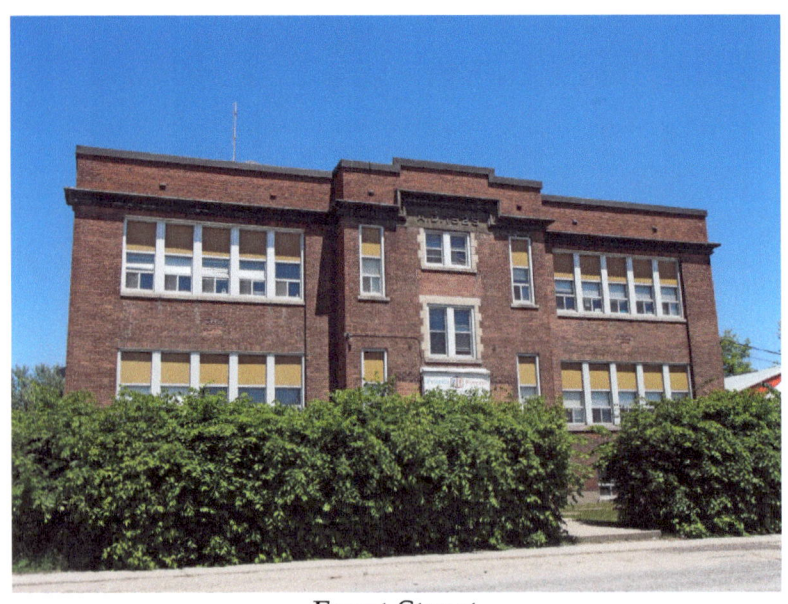

Front Street

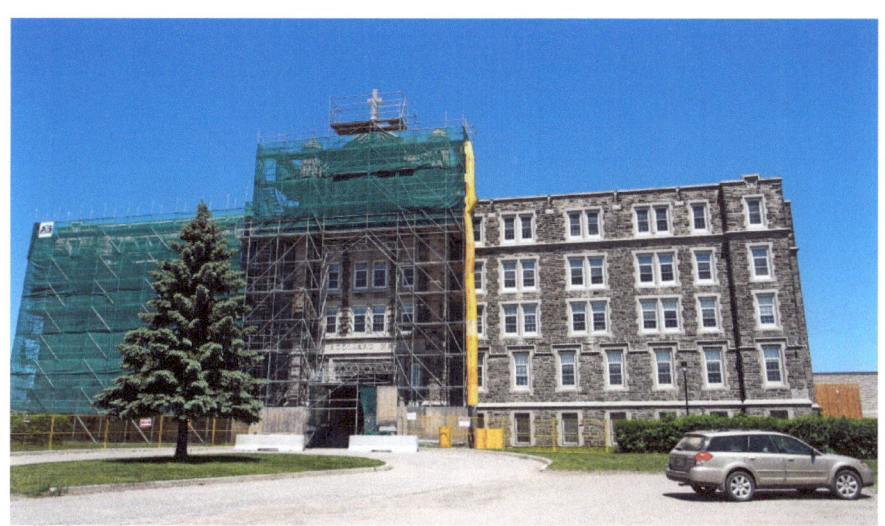

1000 High Street, former Scollard Hall Boys' College - Features of this building are the twin turrets on either side of the projecting frontispiece, the symmetrical organization of the design, and the heavy massing achieved through the use of split-faced cut stone laid in a random coursed pattern. All window and door openings, including trim elements, are framed in smooth-faced cut stone. The original structure was named in honor of Bishop Scollard.

The building was constructed in 1930 as a Catholic high school for male students. In 1985, St. Joseph's College (high school for girls) merged with the original Scollard Hall Boys' College, thus becoming the present St. Joseph-Scollard Hall Catholic Secondary School of the Nipissing Parry-Sound Catholic District School Board.

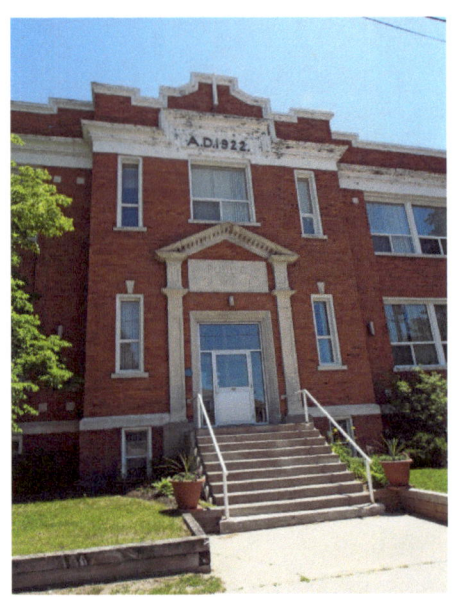

380 McPhail Street - Dr. Carruthers Public School opened in January of 1922. It was named in honor of Dr. J.B. Carruthers, one of the city's pioneer medical doctors. He was an avid musician and during his spare time he visited the local schools to teach the students music.

The exterior of the original three brick sections of the school have a continuous cornice, a varied parapet, and a triangular pediment canopy suspended above the front entrance.

The school closed in 2002 and became an apartment building. The exterior of the building retains its school character. Dr. Carruthers Public School had a rich history and strong family ties as it served a local neighborhood for over seventy-five years.

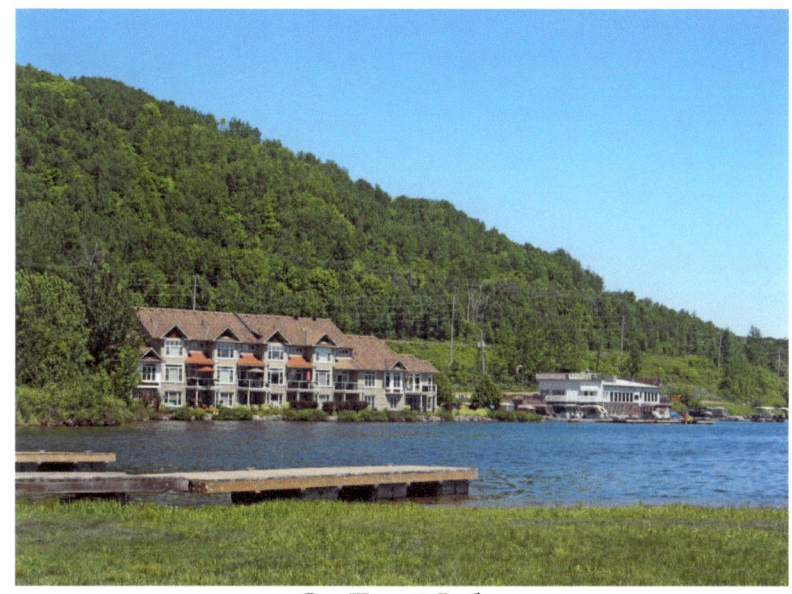

On Trout Lake

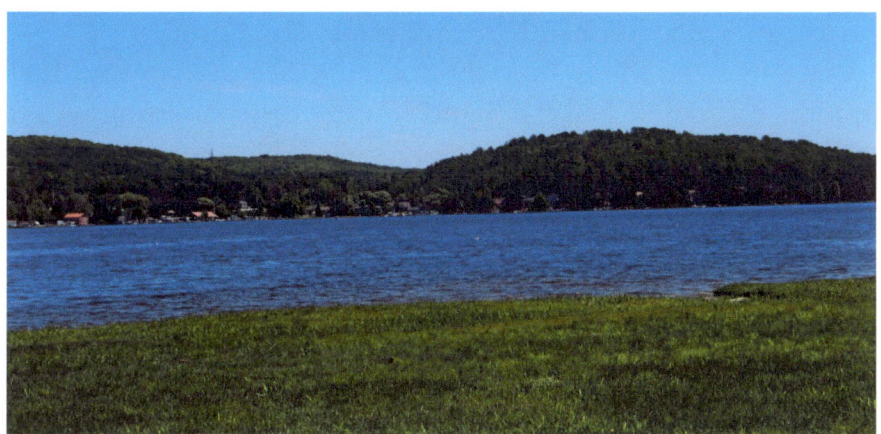

Trout Lake

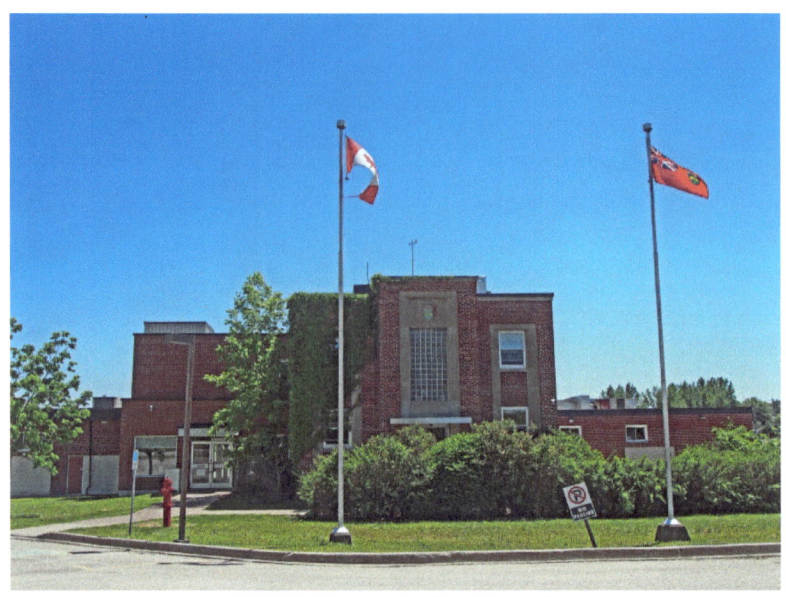

3301 Trout Lake Road

3301 Trout Lake Road - Ministry of Natural Resources and Forestry (MNRF) Building - This property was first home to Milne Lumber Company. The Milne family moved to North Bay from Trout Creek in 1896 and established lumber operations here. Milne Lumber operations ceased around 1940 and it is estimated that the 'Lands and Forests' building was erected within the next decade.

The main building is comprised of red brick with concrete lintels. The coat of arms crest is located above the main entrance, which gives the building the unmistakable prominence of an official government building.

Although the Ministry has undergone a few name and structural changes, it has withstood the test of time and remains functional under the same use as when first constructed.

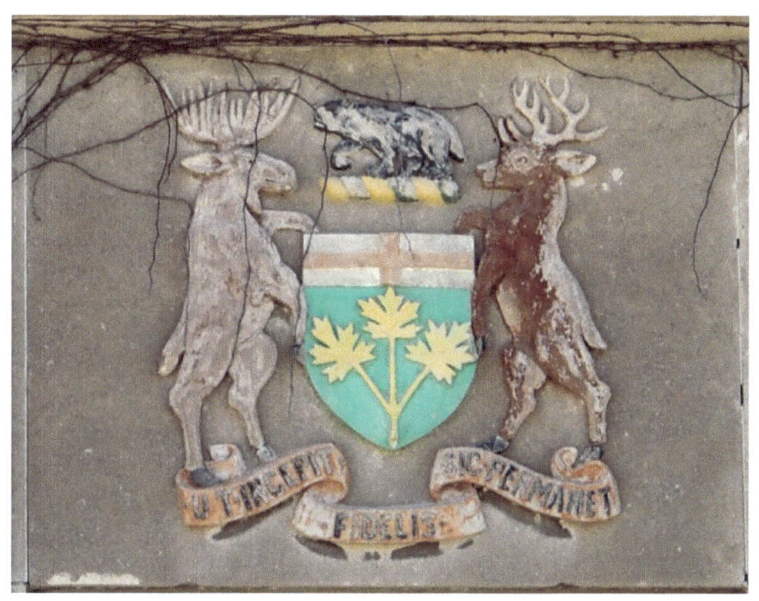

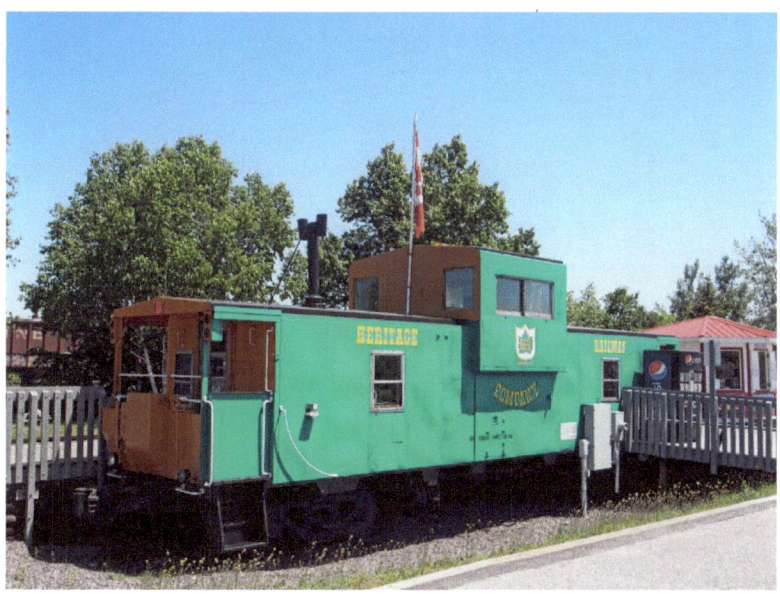

Heritage Train

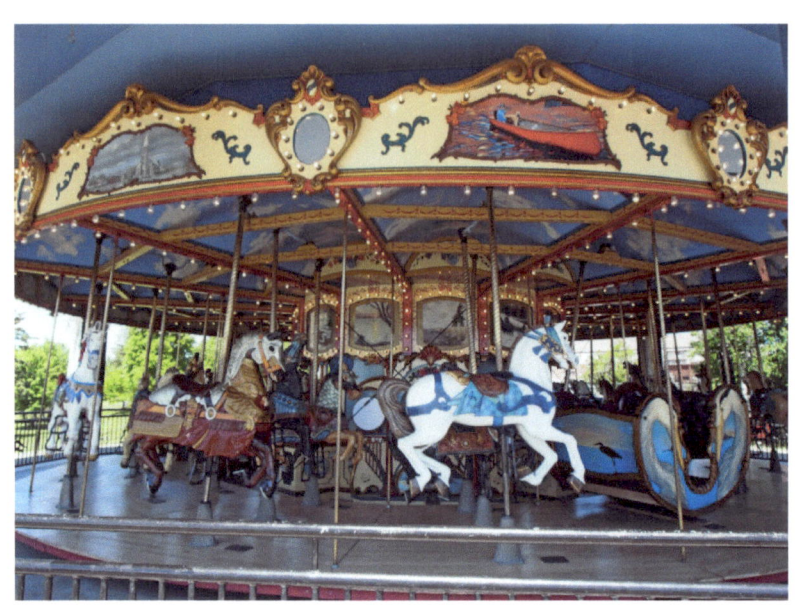

North Bay Heritage Carousel

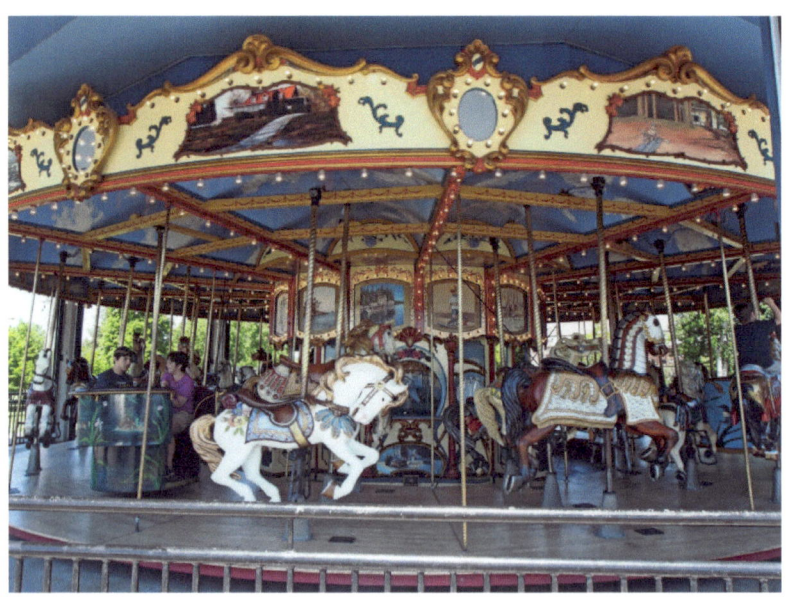

Todd Goings of Marion, Ohio, was contacted to rebuild a 1908 Herschell-Spillman mechanism. Chuck Kaparich of Missoula, Montana carved twenty-eight horses and the North Bay Wood Carvers carved nine. The horses were put up for adoption as well as other parts of the carousel in order to raise funds to pay for the horses, and to paint and furbish the Carousel.

Local artists were approached to paint thirty-three horses and twenty-eight original paintings of local scenes. A rocking chariot, stationary chariot, spinning tub and band organ were carved using local designs that reflect the wildlife of Northern Ontario. The carousel was assembled by its dedicated volunteers.

The Winter Wonderland Carousel opened in Grand style on July 1st, 2005 during a well-attended Canada Day celebration.

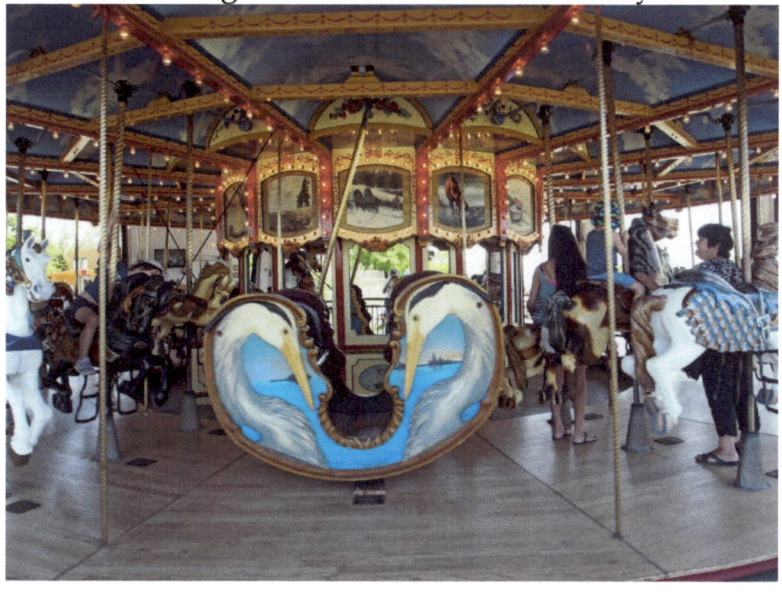

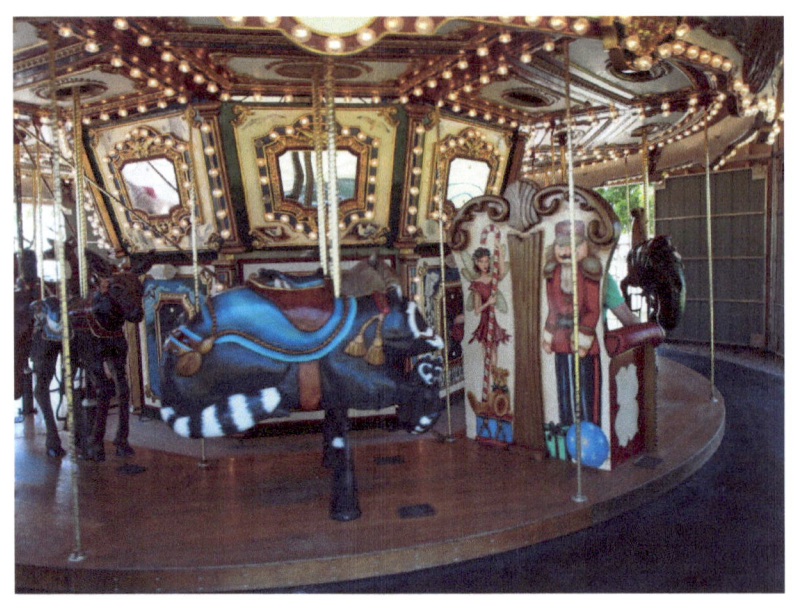

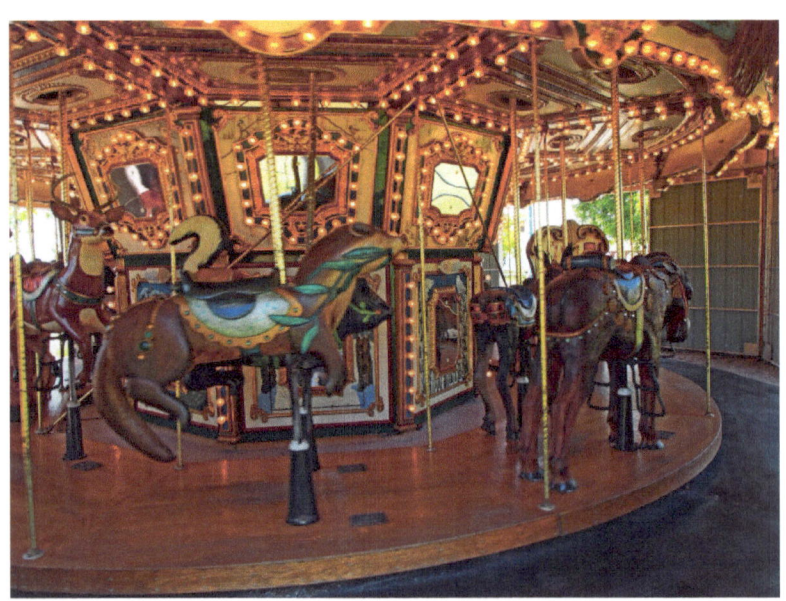

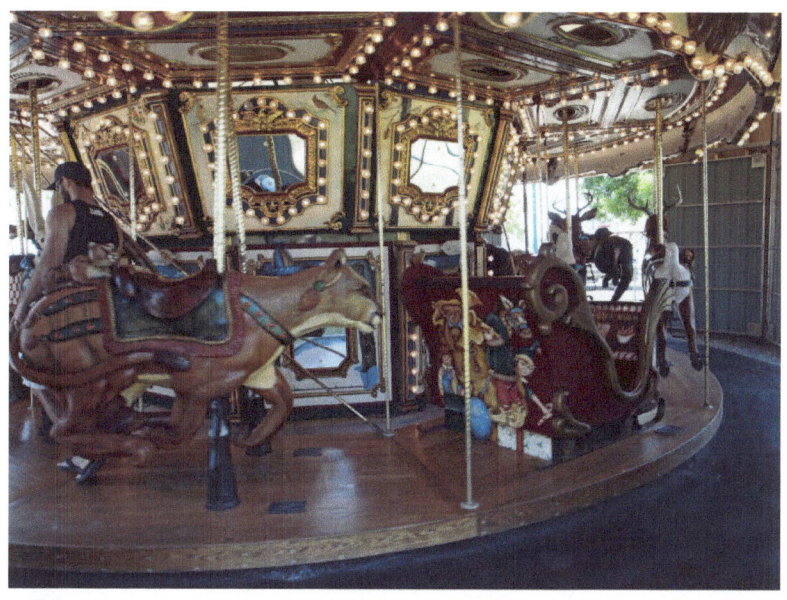

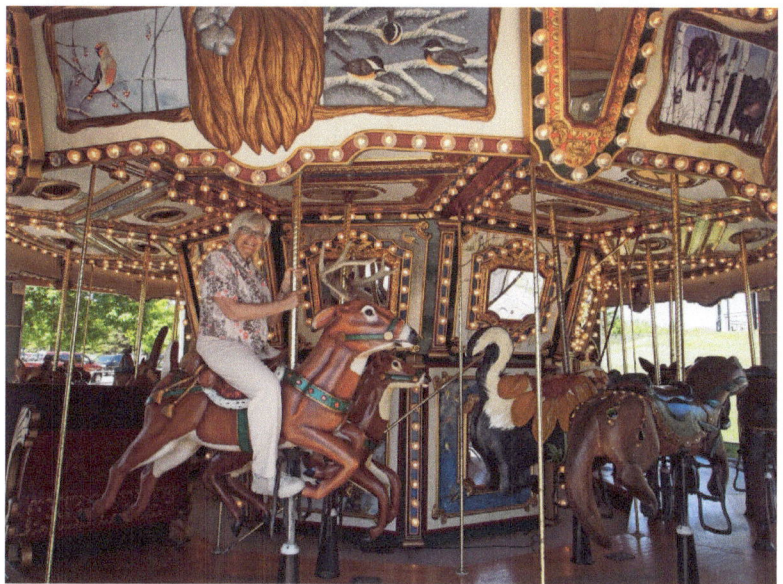

The author is riding on a deer. The other animals include a fox, black bear, mountain lion, moose, otter, beaver, skunk, chipmunk, wolf, racoon, rabbit, a mythical hippocampus, and Santa's Sleigh.

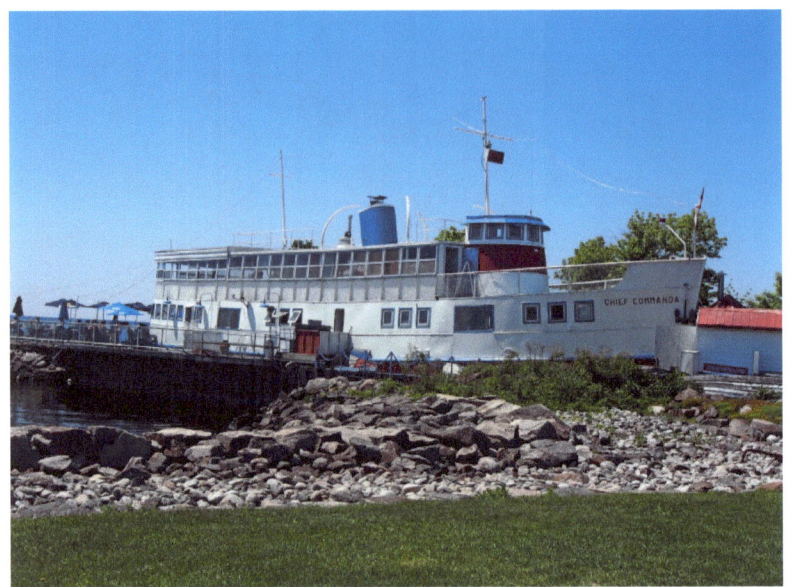

The *Chief Commanda*, powered by two eight cylinder diesel engines was launched in 1946. It carried supplies and vacationers to resorts on Lake Nipissing and the French River which for the most part were only accessible by water.

Preserved and sitting in dry dock, *Chief Commanda* operates as a seasonal restaurant and waterfront attraction.

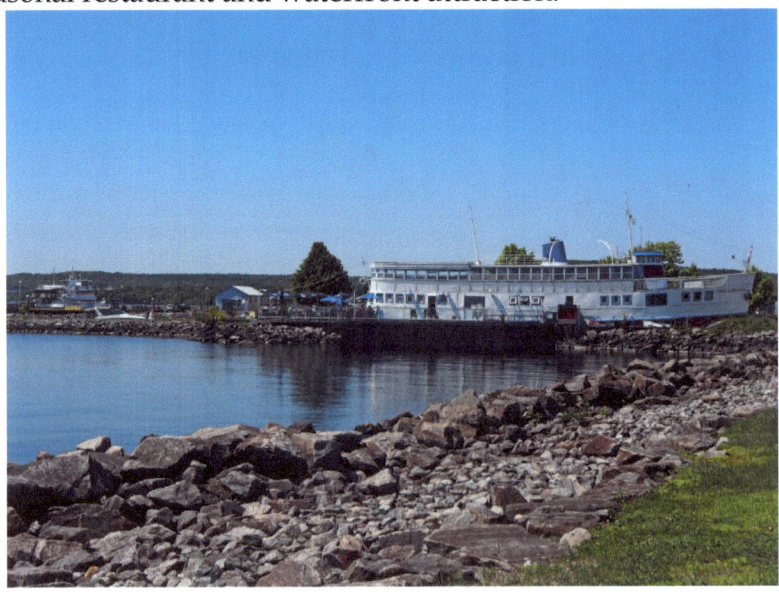

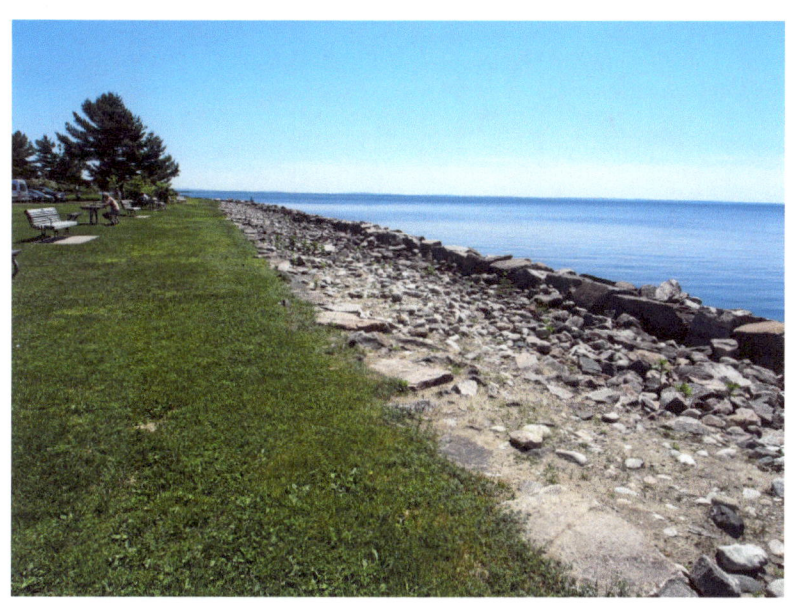

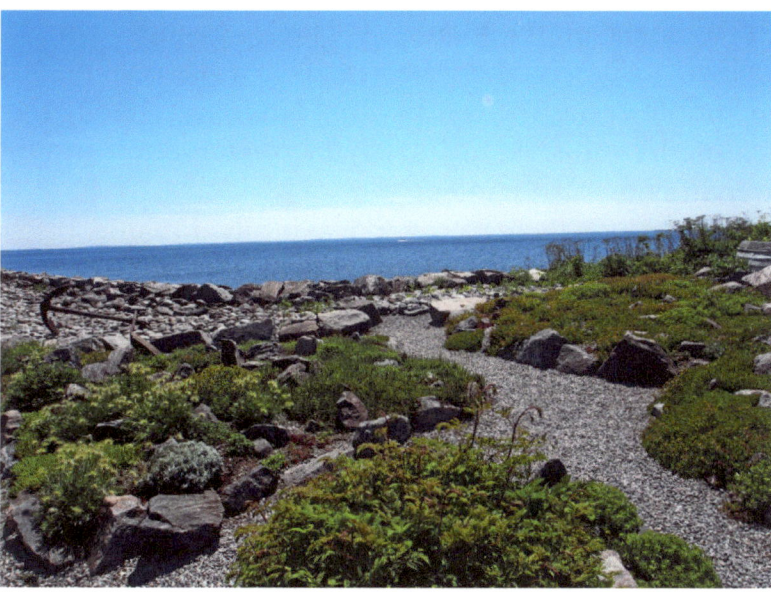

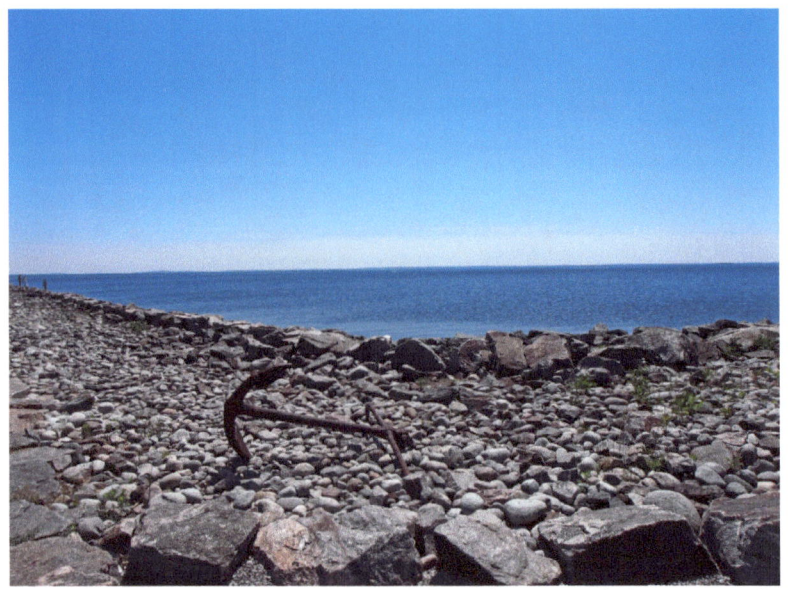

Lake Nipissing is a large lake about 65 kilometres by 25 kilometres. Five islands about ten kilometres offshore from North Bay make up the Manitous. The Nipissings (a branch of the Ojibway tribe) lived on the islands in a seasonal migration. In the middle of the 17th century, the Nipissings had to face the raiding Iroquois. At times they faced starvation and the unforgiving northern winters.

The islands have basswood, ash, silver maple, birch, cedar, burr oak, and sugar maple trees. There are many species of birds including the Great Blue Heron, and ospreys.

The islands are now a Provincial Nature Reserve

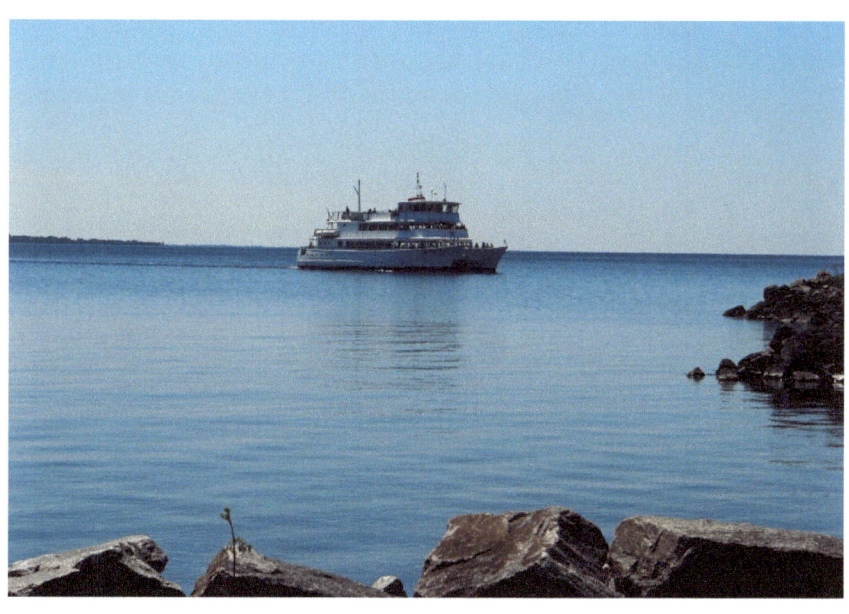

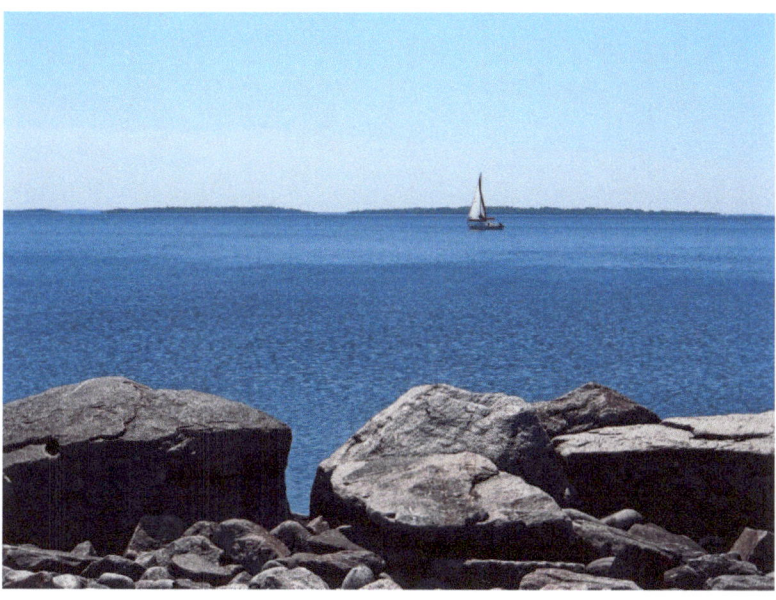

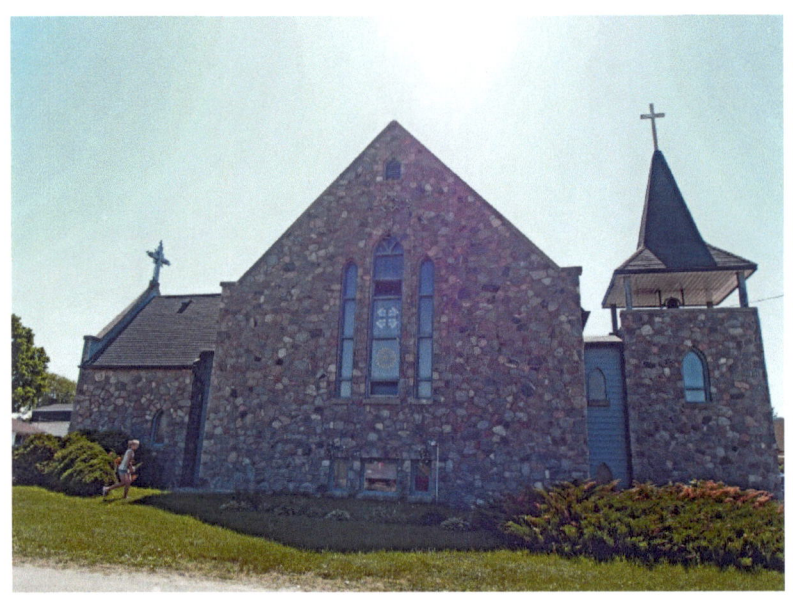

146 Beth Street – Holy Name of Jesus Roman Catholic Church

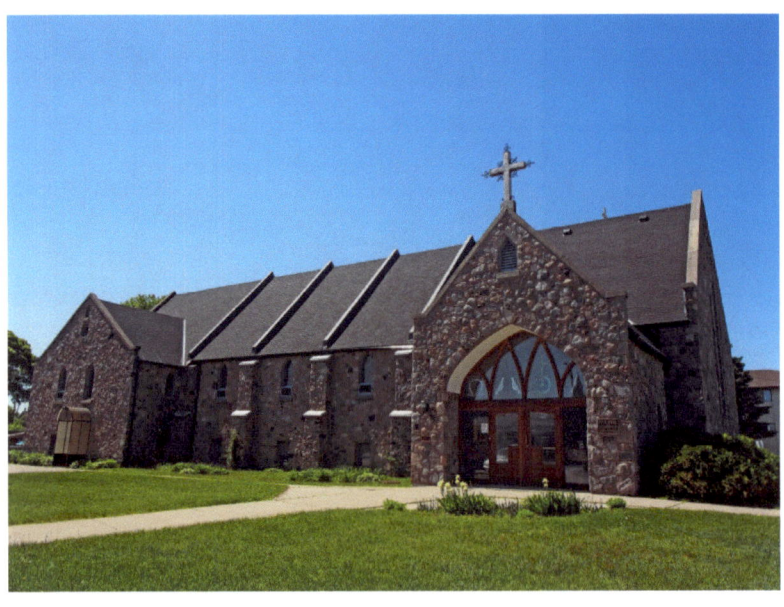

Building Styles

Edwardian, 1900-1930 – This style bridges the ornate and elaborate styles of the Victorian era and the simplified styles of the 20th century. Edwardian Classicism provided simple, balanced facades, simple rooflines, dormer windows, large front porches, and smooth brick surfaces. Voussoirs and keystones are used sparingly and are understated. Finials and cresting are absent. Cornice brackets and braces are block-like and openings have flat arches or plain stone lintels.

Georgian, before 1860 – This style began with the British King Georges in the 18th century. These buildings have balanced facades around a central door, medium-pitched gable roofs, and small paned windows.

Gothic Revival, 1830-1890 – These decorative buildings have sharply-pitched gables with highly detailed verge boards, pointed-arch window openings, and dichromatic brickwork. It is a common style in Ontario.

Neo-Classical, 1810-1850 – This style was a direct result of the War of 1812. Many Upper Canadians returning from the war with the United States were second or third generation Loyalists who had inherited land and means from their forefathers. Once the conflict had passed, they had the money and the time to expand their holdings and indulge their architectural whims. Both residential and commercial buildings were constructed on the traditional Georgian plan, but they had a new gaiety and light-heartedness. Detailing became more refined, delicate, and elegant.

Romanesque Revival, 1880-1910 – This style hearkens back to medieval architecture of the 11th and 12th centuries with a heavy appearance, blocky towers and rounded arches.

Tudor Revival – exposed timbers with stucco infill, multi-paned windows.

Other Books by Barbara Raue

Coins of Gold
Arrows, Indians and Love
The Life and Times of Barbara
The Cromwell Family Book
Laura Secord Discovered
Daddy Where Are You?

Montana Series
Book 1: Montana Dream
Book 2: Life on the Montana Frontier
Book 3: Montana to Boston and Back
Book 4: Montana Sons Go to War
Book 5: Montana Sons Return from War

Donaldson Series
Book 1: Rite of Passage
Book 2: Rite of Marriage

© 2021 by Barbara Raue - All the photos in this book have been taken with my cameras. I own the rights to them.

Barbara is The Authority on Saving Our History One Photo at a Time. She is pursuing her interest in photography and architecture by preserving a record through photos of old buildings from the 1800s and 1900s with their unique architecture. Enjoy the beautiful architecture in the comfort of your living room. Dream about what it was like in those by-gone days. Dream about what it was like to live in a mansion like one of those in this book.

Barbara Raue, a wife, mother and grandmother, is an avid reader and writer. She has researched and compiled several family histories. In 2010, Barbara published her book "Coins of Gold," which celebrates the courageous life of her mother, May Todd. Barbara's second book is a historical fiction "Arrows, Indians and Love" which takes place in Boonesborough, Kentucky during the time of Daniel Boone. In 2013, Barbara published *The Cromwell Family Book* in which she traces her ancestry generations back into Great Britain. Her second novel is called *Laura Secord Discovered,* in which the story of Laura's service during the War of 1812 is shared. Barbara's memoir is titled *Daddy Where Are You?* It tells of her life growing up without a father. Five novels in the Montana Series have been published, *Montana Dream, Life on the Montana Frontier, Montana to Boston and Back, Montana Sons Go to War,* and *Montana Sons Return from War.* The Donaldson series of two novels is available: *Rite of Passage* and *Rite of Marriage.*

This is a link to Barbara's website to view all of her books
http://barbararaue.ca

www.ingramcontent.com/pod-product-compliance
Lightning Source LLC
Chambersburg PA
CBHW041941240526
45473CB00033B/175